lonely planet

NEW YORK CITY

John Garry

Scale cloud-piercing towers for panoramic views. Catch a ferry to tree-topped harbor islands. Open doors to grand buildings built for royalty. Pay your respects at monuments honoring local legends. Deck yourself out with fashion from unique boutiques. Savor the array of global dining options. Sip craft cocktails inside hidden speakeasies. Feel the jolt of excitement as curtains rise on a Broadway show. Walk streets glittering with bright lights from skyscrapers.

This is New York City.

TURN THE PAGE AND START PLANNING YOUR NEXT BEST TRIP →

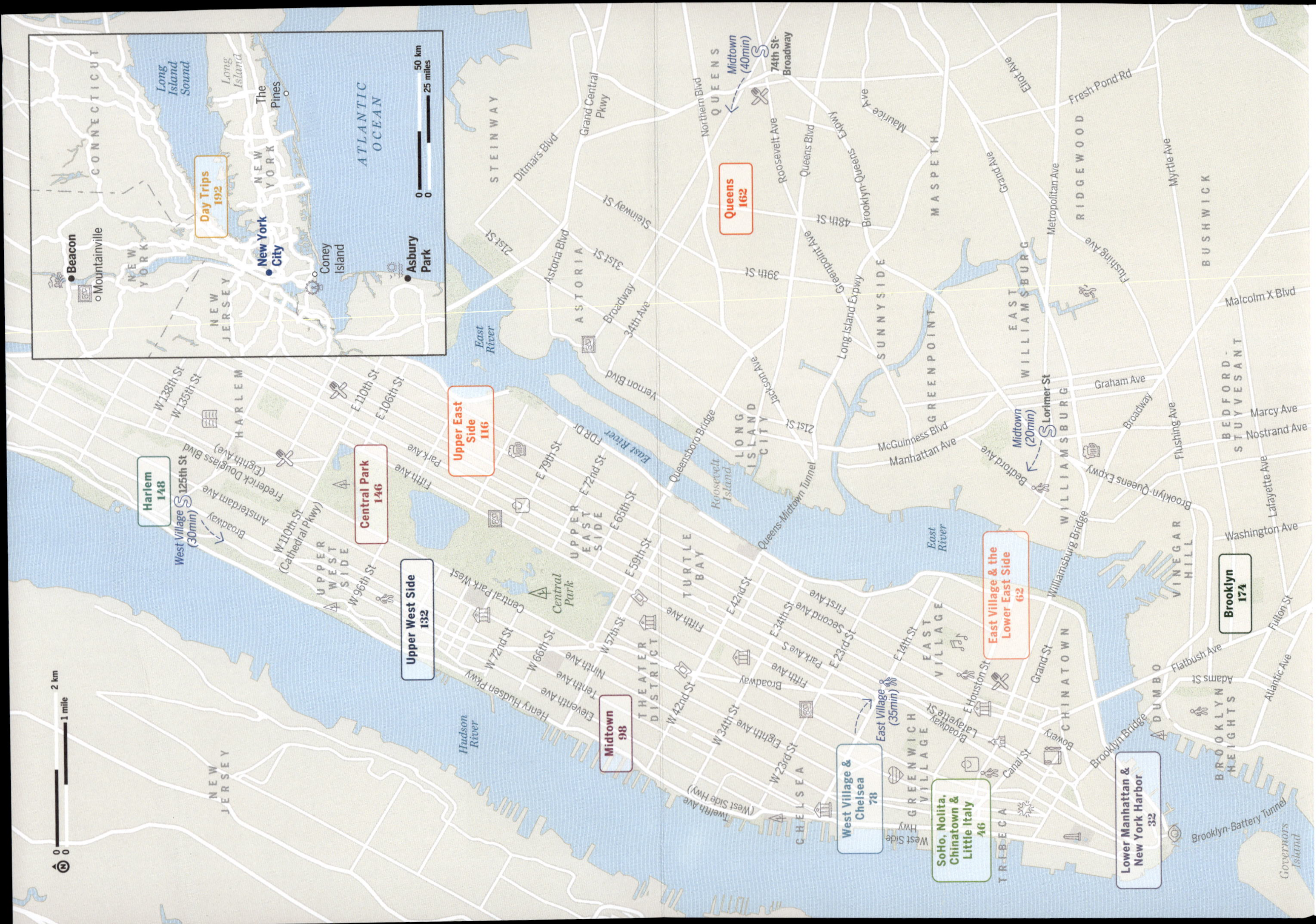

Meet our writer

This is the 2nd edition of Lonely Planet's *Experience New York City* guidebook, updated with new material by John Garry. Writers on the previous edition whose work also appears in this book are included below.

John Garry
@garryjohnfrancis

John Garry is a writer, teacher, biker, urban wanderer, avid museum-goer and long-time theater nerd who eats out way too much in Brooklyn, where he lives.

Contributing Writers

Harmony Difo, Dana Givens, Deepa Lakshmin

Previous spread Brooklyn Bridge (p180) and Manhattan

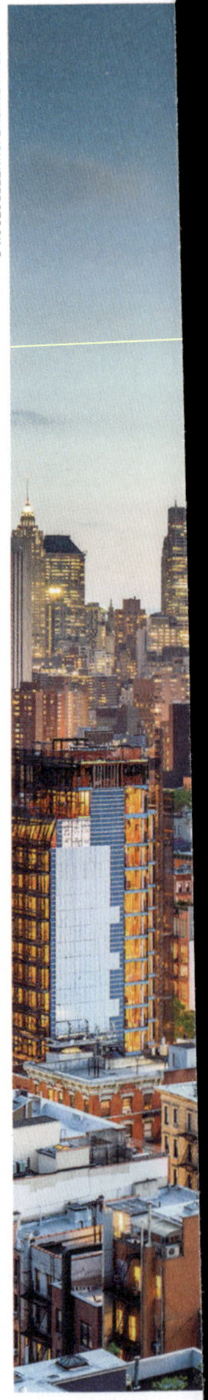

Financial District, Lower Manhattan (p32)

Contents

TERELYUK/SHUTTERSTOCK ©

Central Park (p146)

AMAZING OBSERVATORIES

All five of NYC's boroughs are visible from One World Observatory. (p39)

The Edge boasts the western hemisphere's highest outdoor sky deck. (p113)

1860 steps link the Empire State Building's ground-floor and 102nd floor observation deck – along with 73 elevators. (p112)

SKYLINE **VIEWS**

Seeing New York's steely skyscraper forest is spectacular, but appreciating its immensity can be challenging if you're caught wandering through Manhattan's street-level concrete canyons. Head instead to places that offer unique perspectives – tower-top observatories, river bridges and waterfronts in Brooklyn, where views of Manhattan's skyline dazzle in the distance.

Left New York City's skyline
Right Billionaires' Row
Below One World Trade Center (p39)

→ TOP-DOLLAR TOWERS

NYC's most prominent collection of towers compete for attention along 57th St in Midtown, dubbed Billionaires' Row. It's home to some of the city's most expensive real estate and expansive views.

JOHN PENNEY/SHUTTERSTOCK ©

↓ TALL COMPETITION

There are over a dozen skyscrapers in NYC defined as 'supertalls' – buildings exceeding 984ft in height. The tallest? One World Trade Center, soaring 1776ft into the clouds.

RIGHT: PIT STOCK/SHUTTERSTOCK ©; LEFT: TTSTUDIO/SHUTTERSTOCK ©

FIRST OF ITS KIND

Manhattan's first skyscraper, the slender Tower Building, shot above the skyline in 1889. It only stood 11 stories and was demolished in 1914, eventually replaced by a 37-story office compound.

Views from Every Angle

▸ **Cruise to Liberty Island, where the Statue of Liberty gazes at FiDi's gleaming towers from afar.** (p42)

▸ **Grab a bench on the Brooklyn Heights Promenade as the sun sets behind Manhattan.** (p182)

▸ **Sip cocktails while soaking up East River views from the 18th-floor Panorama Room.** (p129)

▸ **Climb above Central Park's treeline at the Met's Cantor Roof Garden Bar and ogle Midtown's towers.** (p123)

↖ MIGRATION STATION

New York City sits along the Atlantic Flyway, a north-south route for migrating birds connecting Greenland to the Caribbean. In spring and autumn, join birdwatchers in Central Park's North Woods (p147) as hundreds of species flap through.

GREEN **SPACES**

For a city called the 'concrete jungle,' NYC is covered in greenery. New York's parks decorate 29,000 acres at over 1900 sites across all five boroughs. There's a sizable collection designed by 19th-century landscape architects Frederick Law Olmsted and Calvert Vaux, industrial waterfronts repurposed as adventure pads and even a defunct railway revived as a popular promenade. Escape city stressors by communing with the sublime.

Left North Woods (p147), Central Park
Right Brooklyn Bridge Park (p178)
Below Hudson River Greenway

→ REIMAGINED RIVERFRONT

NYC's piers buzzed with business in the late 19th- to mid-20th centuries but became derelict wastelands by the 1980s. They are now public spaces, such as Brooklyn Bridge Park (p178), a shining example of urban renewal.

ELENAGB/SHUTTERSTOCK ©

BARD AMONG BUDS

Fantastic free events occur in parks throughout summer, including Shakespeare in the Park, a star-studded summer series hosted by the Public at the Delacorte Theater.

▶ See p145 for more information

RIGHT: HERE NOW/SHUTTERSTOCK ©; LEFT: JOE JOSEPHS/SHUTTERSTOCK ©

↑ SERIOUS CYCLING

Join NYC's pedal party on the 13-mile Hudson River Greenway, a bike path that crosses through Hudson River Park, Riverside Park, Fort Washington Park and Fort Tryon.

▶ Learn more about Hudson River Park (p82)

More Trees, Please

▶ **Go wild in Central Park, where serpentine paths wind through 843 acres of forests and meadows.** (p146)

▶ **Take a five-minute ferry ride to trade traffic-logged streets for the car-free promenades of Governors Island.** (p36)

▶ **Pause among stems and statues around Elizabeth Street Garden – a hidden oasis amid Nolita's boutiques.** (p51)

▶ **Walk down the pretty-in-pink Cherry Esplanade in Brooklyn Botanic Garden when blossoms bloom in spring.** (p187)

INTERNATIONAL EXCHANGE

NYC must-eats reflect the city's multicultural heritage and evolution: bagels arrived via Jewish Polish newcomers in the 19th century – and now Korean immigrants make some of the city's best at Absolute Bagels (p144). Pizza comes from Naples, Italy; sample coal-fired perfection at Lombardi's (p60), NYC's oldest pizzeria.

NOSH IN NEW YORK

Over 23,000 restaurants call NYC home. Michelin-starred fine diners, retro luncheonettes, food carts with global flair and pop-up markets featuring innovative treats: if you can imagine it, New York likely makes it. Don't leave without trying the Big Apple essentials – pizza, bagels, a pastrami on rye and the coveted bodega BEC (bacon, egg and cheese) – and be sure to visit immigrant enclaves to find classics from foreign lands.

Left Food trucks Right Chinatown (p54)
Below Dirt Candy dish (p76)

→ RESTAURANT RESERVATIONS

Popular establishments require reservations, sometimes a month in advance. Even for lesser-known spots, it's helpful to prebook a table and ensure you get a seat – particularly on busy weekend evenings.

↓ PLANT-BASED, PLEASE

Meat-free eaters can rejoice: there's Michelin-starred vegan at Dirt Candy (p76), Southern-style soul food at VeganHood (p160) and the vegan patty at Superiority Burger (p76) might be the best in NYC.

RESTAURANT 'WEEK'

For one month in summer (July and August) and winter (January and February), the city's finer restaurants offer promotions on prix-fixe meals – some under $50.

▶ nyctourism.com/restaurant-week

Eat Around the World

▶ **Take a trip to South India with the assortment of curries and chutneys at Michelin-starred Semma.** (p96)

▶ **Dine on savory dumplings and sweet buns from tiny food counters sprinkled around Chinatown.** (p54)

▶ **Explore the globe one food truck at a time on a delectable Jackson Heights food tour.** (p166)

▶ **Pretend it's 1948 while sipping egg creams in a Lexington Candy Shop booth.** (p124)

HOLY ARCHITECTURE

The yet-to-be-completed Cathedral Church of St John the Divine (p161) is the largest cathedral in the US, covering over 120,000 sq ft. It also houses the third-largest rose window in the world, created with over 10,000 pieces of glass.

INTRIGUING **INTERIORS**

There's plenty of eye candy on NYC's streets, but wait until you see what's hiding behind closed doors. Glorious train stations entice harried commuters to stay for a while. Gilded mansions-turned-museums invite visitors to imagine life as 19th-century millionaires. There are celestial frescoes, stained-glass windows, contemporary structures that look like canyons and theaters where the building steals the show. Take a peek.

Left Rose Reading Room, New York Public Library (p109) **Right** New Amsterdam Theatre **Below** Frick Collection (p127)

→ STARS OF THE STAGE

Proscenium arches in Broadway theaters are so ornate they can distract from performances – though they are nothing compared to the Park Avenue Armory (p131), a theater with rooms designed by Louis Comfort Tiffany and more.

PIT STOCK/SHUTTERSTOCK ©

NATURE'S INFLUENCE

The 2023 addition at American Museum of Natural History, the Gilder Center, looks like Navajo Sandstone smack dab in urban Manhattan. The cost to recreate nature? $465 million.

▶ For more information, see p138

RIGHT: MARCOBRIVIO.PHOTOGRAPHY/SHUTTERSTOCK ©; LEFT: WANGKUN JIA/SHUTTERSTOCK ©

↑ MAGNIFICENT MANSION

Fifth Ave along Central Park was once home to NYC's Gilded Age elite, lined with extravagant mansions like the Frick Collection.

▶ Tour the Frick Collection galleries (p127) for a taste of how they lived.

Tour the Decor

▶ **Look skyward inside the Main Concourse at Grand Central Terminal to see the starlit ceiling.** (p108)

▶ **Get lost in the pink clouds decorating the Rose Reading Room fresco at New York Public Library.** (p109)

▶ **Spiral up the Guggenheim's concrete ribbon, a cream-colored masterpiece by architect Frank Lloyd Wright.** (p131)

▶ **Sit in a pew at the Museum at Eldridge Street and admire the synagogue's stained glass.** (p71)

POWERFUL MEMORIALS

Over 1000 memorials ornament NYC, popping up in parks and along sidewalks as busts, fountains, figures and abstract sculptures – each a stone or metal memory of New York's greatest hopes, darkest days and notable heroes. Some loom large, like the Statue of Liberty, while others can be easily overlooked. Get curious – even small monuments tell sweeping stories.

LEFT: LEV RADIN/SHUTTERSTOCK ©; BOTTOM: FELIX LIPOV/SHUTTERSTOCK ©

→ CONVERSATION STARTER

NYC has spent the past decade re-examining old monuments and the painful history they symbolize. Some have been yanked from view, while others – like a statue of Christopher Columbus near Central Park – remain controversial talking points.

Noble Stories

- **Celebrate LGBTIQ+ activists at Stonewall National Monument, site of a game-changing uprising in 1969.** (p91)
- **Pay your respects at the National September 11 Memorial, where Manhattan's cacophony turns into quiet contemplation.** (p39)
- **Give your regards to George M Cohan, the show biz song-and-dance man grinning above Times Square.** (p104)

BAD BUSINESS

You'll find 20-plus memorials scattered around the Battery's 25 acres – including the bronze-and-granite Netherland Monument (p39), commemorating the Dutch 'purchase' of 'Manahatta' from the Indigenous Lenape.

Top Stonewall National Monument (p91)
Bottom Columbus Circle

SHOP UNTIL **YOU DROP**

Make room in your closet. Between vintage bazaars, upscale boutiques, novelty stores and big-name brands, you could leave NYC with an entirely new wardrobe. SoHo is the city's fashion capital, but there are plenty of other neighborhoods worth window shopping. Williamsburg stores range from avant-garde to upscale, the Lower East Side is stacked with trendsetters, and pop-up markets showcase local artisans all over the city.

LEFT: DW LABS INCORPORATED/SHUTTERSTOCK ©; BOTTOM: RANDY DUCHAINE / ALAMY STOCK PHOTO ©

↑ HOLIDAY MARKETS

Every December, a series of Christmas markets take over parks throughout Manhattan, including Union Square, where you'll find over 100 vendors selling unique gifts and street food. It's a cheery way to get into the holiday spirit.

Unique Shopping

- **Wander between SoHo and Nolita, where local makers sell clothing from jewel-box boutiques.** (p50)
- **Skip down Orchard St, where art galleries, book stores and vintage shops compete for attention.** (p72)
- **Traipse the shop-lined streets of South Street Seaport to the Tin Building, a food market and grocer.** (p40)

↙ CITY SWAG

Search for authentic NYC memorabilia, like FDNY caps and subway shirts at CityStore (p44) in Lower Manhattan. For playful graphic fashion inspired by New York, stop by Only NY (p77).

Top Union Square Christmas market
Bottom NYC memorabilia

IMBIBE IN STYLE

The 'city that doesn't sleep' actually calls it quits at 4am, when sales of alcohol are prohibited, and you'll likely be happy it does. Mixologists craft cocktails in Manhattan, hop heads beeline to Brooklyn breweries and clubs in Queens attract late-night revelry. After splashing between speakeasies or spending all night on the dance floor, you're going to crave a cat nap.

↑ COFFEE CULTURE

Not into alcohol? Over 3000 coffee shops fuel NYC's hustling hordes. There are plenty of local java joints: try SEY Coffee (p191), which roasts their beans like chemists, and Abraço (p76), where espressos are best paired with olive oil cake.

Beer, Booze & Wine

▸ **Order flowery and funky brews at Grimm Artisanal Ales, best enjoyed on the rooftop terrace.** (p190)

▸ **Slide into a booth at Long Island Bar, serving cocktails created by the Cosmo's inventor.** (p190)

▸ **Belt musical medleys with boozed-up Broadway fans at piano bar Marie's Crisis.** (p97)

SPEAKEASY INSPIRED

Prohibition in the 1920s forced spirits-serving establishments to go undercover – called 'speakeasies' for the quiet voices patrons used to ensure bars went undetected.

▸ Visit PDT (p75) to recall the era.

Top SEY Coffee (p191)
Bottom Marie's Crisis (p97)

FUN FOR THE **FAMILY**

New York is the ultimate kid's playground. Roll through Central Park's green fields, see Broadway shows with Disney pedigree or spend a day riding waterfront roller coasters. There's also a glut of immersive museums catering to young minds, ensuring NYC is as educational as it is fun. There are plenty of ways to keep things cheap, too. No one is getting bored.

LEFT: RESUL MUSLU/SHUTTERSTOCK ©; BOTTOM: NURPHOTO/GETTY IMAGES ©

→ DUELING CAROUSELS

Settle this serious Manhattan–Brooklyn rivalry: which borough has the better carousel? Twirl around the fish-tastic SeaGlass Carousel (p45) in Lower Manhattan then go for a pony ride on the vintage Jane's Carousel (p180) in Brooklyn Bridge Park.

Kid Approved

- **Stand in the shadow of dinosaur skeletons at the American Museum of Natural History.** (p138)
- **Wave to Kermit the Frog at the Jim Henson exhibit at Museum of the Moving Image.** (p169)
- **Skip among the flowers at Brooklyn Botanic Garden, where entrance is free for children under 12.** (p187)

← SEEING LIVE THEATER

Seeing Broadway shows is an expensive family endeavor, but there are plenty of other affordable options. See what's on at the New Victory (p103), a fantastic theater aimed at young audiences, then tour the immersive, kid-friendly Museum of Broadway (p102).

Top Jane's Carousel (p180)
Bottom American Museum of Natural History (p138)

Free in Central Park

Head to Manhattan's green lungs for Shakespeare in the Park and SummerStage's free concert series.

▶ cityparksfoundation.org/summerstage

▶ Shakespeare in the Park (p145)

Mermaid Parade

An artsy, eclectic crowd dons nautical costumes to flip their fins down Surf Ave during this Coney Island summer-solstice celebration in mid-June.

▶ coneyisland.com/mermaidparade

↗ Puerto Rican Day Parade

Sounds of salsa and reggaeton enliven Fifth Ave as the city's Boricua contingency bops along repping Caribbean pride in early June.

▶ nprdpinc.org

LGBTIQ+ Pride

NYC rolls out the rainbow carpet in all five boroughs throughout June. Events culminate in a flamboyant Manhattan Pride parade.

▶ nycpride.org

JUNE

Average daytime max (June): 79°F
Days of rainfall: 11

JULY

New York in SUMMER

↘ Fourth of July

Independence Day sizzles with innumerable BBQs and Coney Island's infamous hot dog eating contest. The grand finale: fireworks.

▶ Coney Island p200

↖ Afropunk

This multi-genre music festival celebrates Black culture and music with a weekend of live performances, funky fashion and craft markets at the end of August.

▶ afropunk.com

AUGUST

Average daytime max (July): 85°F
Days of rainfall: 10

Average daytime max (August): 83°F
Days of rainfall: 9

↙ Beaches

Summer's dog days in August are best spent oceanside. Take a trip to the Jersey Shore or hang local at Jacob Riis.

▶ Jersey Shore (p204)
▶ Jacob Riis (p173; pictured)

BRIC Celebrate Brooklyn!

Free concerts, movies and other performances erupt at Prospect Park's Lena Horne Bandshell all summer long.

▶ bricartsmedia.org

Packing Notes

Dress for hot, muggy weather but bring layers – most businesses pump the air-conditioning.

Labor Day Weekend

Many New Yorkers take their last gasp of summer vacation at the beach; folks from the Caribbean march in the West Indian Day Parade.

▶ wiadcacarnival.org

Fashion Week

In mid-September top designers take their spring collections to runway shows attended by celebrity style hounds and trendsetters.

▶ nyfw.com

Feast of San Gennaro

Little Italy's Mulberry St dresses up in red, white and green for an 11-day block party honoring the patron saint of Naples.

▶ sangennaronyc.org

↑ Upstate Leaf Peeping

Autumn leaves turn amber and gold in forests north of NYC – ideal for visiting outdoor sculpture park Storm King.

▶ stormking.org

▶ Storm King (p196)

SEPTEMBER

Average daytime max (September): 76°F
Days of rainfall: 9

OCTOBER

New York in FALL

BAM Next Wave Festival

From October to January, avant-garde dance, music, theater and opera performances take over the Brooklyn Academy of Music, highlighting daring artistry.

▶ bam.org

↗ Village Halloween Parade

Skeletons and spiderwebs decorate West Village stoops – a prelude to All Hallows Eve, when New Yorkers get sartorially spooky.

▶ halloween-nyc.com

▶ Greet the Village's Ghosts (p94)

↗ New York City Marathon

In early November daring runners tackle a 26.2-mile course that zigzags through all five boroughs and ends in Central Park.

▶ nyrr.org/tcsnycmarathon

Average daytime max (October): 65°F
Days of rainfall: 10

NOVEMBER

Average daytime max (November): 54°F
Days of rainfall: 9

Thanksgiving Day Parade

Massive helium-filled balloons float above kicking Rockettes, high-school marching bands and Manhattan crowds during Macy's annual celebration in November.

▶ macys.com/s/parade/join-the-parade

↘ Holiday Markets

Between Thanksgiving and Christmas, pop-up markets sell treasures and treats in Union Square, Bryant Park and Columbus Circle.

▶ usqholiday.nyc

↑ New Year's Eve

An army of merrymakers descend on Times Square to ring in the new year and see the iconic ball drop.

▶ timessquarenyc.org

Ice Skating

Join crowds gliding around Manhattan ice-skating rinks at Rockefeller Center, Central Park's Wollman Rink and Bryant Park.

DECEMBER

JANUARY

Average daytime max (December): 44°F
Days of rainfall: 11

New York in WINTER

FROM LEFT: JON HICKS/GETTY IMAGES ©, SYNDI PILAR/SHUTTERSTOCK ©, ERIN CADIGAN/SHUTTERSTOCK ©, SYNDI PILAR/SHUTTERSTOCK ©, BOTTOM: STUART MONK/SHUTTERSTOCK ©

Deals on Hotels

NYC Hotel Week lasts from early January through early February, with discounts available for those who book well in advance.

▶ nyctourism.com/hotel-week-about

↖ NYC Restaurant Week

Tons of restaurants led by world-class chefs offer affordable two- or three-course prix-fixe meals for lunch and dinner.

▶ nyctourism.com/restaurant-week

↑ Lunar New Year

Firecrackers burst in the air, confetti decorates sidewalks and dancing lions bounce throughout Chinatown celebrating the Chinese New Year.

▶ thinkchinatown.org

Average daytime max (January): 39°F
Days of rainfall: 11

FEBRUARY

Average daytime max (February): 42 °F
Days of rainfall: 10

Snow isn't guaranteed. Between 2022 and 2024, New York experienced a 702-day dry spell with no serious accumulation of fluffy stuff.

Weather can turn on a dime, vacillating from below freezing to above 50°F: come prepared for both.

Packing Notes

Come with your warmest coat, hat and gloves – plus a pair of comfortable snow boots.

↓ St Patrick's Day Parade

The world's oldest and longest parade dedicated to Ireland floods Fifth Ave with a sea of green and the sound of bagpipes.

▶ nycstpatricksparade.org

↘ Baseball Season

The Mets (based at Citi Field, Queens) and the Yankees (based at Yankee Stadium, Bronx) kick off the baseball season in April.

▶ mlb.com/yankees

↑ Easter Parade

Every Easter, New Yorkers don fancy, frilly and fantastical bonnets to march along Fifth Ave between 49th and 57th Sts.

MARCH

Average daytime max (March): 50°F
Days of rainfall: 11

APRIL

New York in SPRING

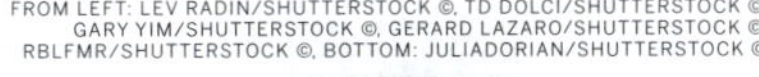

Cherry Blossoms

In April and May, blooming cherry trees throughout NYC beckon crowds to picnic beneath their petals. Brooklyn Botanic Garden grows a splendid collection.

▶ bbg.org

▶ Brooklyn Botanic Garden (p187)

↗ TD Five Boro Bike Tour

Cyclists roll through all five boroughs on a 40-mile bike ride across car-free streets in May.

▶ bike.nyc/events/td-five-boro-bike-tour

Westminster Kennel Club Dog Show

Come May, the prettiest pooch in the pack gets crowned 'Best in Show' at this floofy canine competition in Flushing Meadows-Corona Park, Queens.

▶ westminsterkennelclub.org/westminster-week

↑ Memorial Day

Many New Yorkers skip town to celebrate this three-day weekend in late May – the unofficial start to summer. NYC beaches open for the season.

Average daytime max (April):
60°F
Days of rainfall: 11

MAY

Average daytime max (May):
71°F
Days of rainfall: 12

Daffodils announce the arrival of spring – and allergy season. You may experience symptoms, especially when pollen counts are high. Visit a pharmacy for over-the-counter medication.

Packing Notes

Expect wintry weather through mid-April and hotter days by May. Bring an umbrella, raincoat and layers.

MY PERFECT DAYS IN NEW YORK CITY

By John Garry
@garryjohn francis

DAY 1

Start with a history crash course at the Museum of the City of New York (p131) then saunter to the Metropolitan Museum of Art (p120) to admire select Egyptian and European masterpieces. From there, ramble across Central Park (p146) to the Upper West Side for a square-cut pizza slice from Mama's TOO! (p144). Once you're satiated, hop on a Citi Bike in Riverside Park (p140) and cycle down the Hudson River toward Midtown. Finish with an Off-Broadway show at innovative Playwrights Horizons (p103).

WHY I LOVE NEW YORK CITY

New York City maintains the integrity of its name by never getting old. When I think I've seen it all, the city surprises me most.

STEFAN UGLJEVAREVIC/SHUTTERSTOCK ©

ANNE CZICHOS/SHUTTERSTOCK ©

Above left Citi Bike **Above right** Playwrights Horizons (p103)
Above Brownstones, Brooklyn Heights (p184)

DAY 2

Lust over beautiful brownstones on a morning stroll through Brooklyn Heights (p184) while gobbling a croissant from L'Appartement 4F (p184). Arrive at the Brooklyn Heights Promenade (p182) to survey Manhattan's skyline, then walk across the Brooklyn Bridge (p180) for East River views. Once in Manhattan, eat your way through Chinatown at dumpling-and-bun counters like Fried Dumpling (p54), then cross back to Brooklyn for more food in Williamsburg. Nibble small plates at Michelin-starred Four Horsemen (p190) and end with all-night dancing at Elsewhere (p188).

JUMIS/SHUTTERSTOCK ©

DAY 3

Stroll along the High Line (p84) as the sun rises over contemporary towers, then graze through Chelsea Market (p86) before zipping to the Whitney's permanent 7th-floor collection (p87), packed with New York notables like Hopper and Warhol. Wander through the West Village's maze of streets next, grabbing espresso or wine at cafe-cum-bar St Jardim (p96). Pass through bustling Washington Square Park (p95) en route to dinner at Thai Diner (p60), then roll into the Lower East Side for speakeasy-style cocktails at Attaboy (p77).

BEST UNIQUE MUSEUMS

City Reliquary Admire NYC ephemera. (p191)

Nicholas Roerich Museum Wander the painting-packed brownstone. (p145)

Tenement Museum Explore the history of immigrant life. (p70)

WACKY & WONDERFUL

Russian & Turkish Baths Sweat in basement saunas. (p77)

Joe's Pub Applaud a quirky cabaret. (p61)

Beacon Take a day trip to see outdoor sculpture and minimalist art. (p198)

7 Things to Know About NEW YORK CITY

INSIDER TIPS TO HIT THE GROUND RUNNING

1 There's a Street Grid

Manhattan's streets (increasing in number as they head north) and perpendicular avenues (increasing in number as they head west) define urban life. There's no definitive city center but a mosaic of cultural focal points, each block its own mini-universe. It's also easily navigable – unless you're in the Financial District or West Village. The grid is rational, direct and no-nonsense, just like the typical New Yorker.

2 Bodegas are Havens

Some call them delis. Others call them convenience stores. The proper term is 'bodega' and they are an embodiment of the 'city never sleeps,' often open 24/7. It's technically a store with no more than two cash registers that sells milk and mostly food, but it isn't a specialty store like a butcher. It's a neighborhood lifeline for groceries, beer, lottery tickets, ATMs and the beloved BEC (bacon, egg and cheese), sometimes guarded by a 'bodega cat.'

3 Obey Sidewalk Etiquette

New Yorkers use the sidewalk for commuting – not dawdling. Traffic flows to the right. If you want to pause to check your phone or look up, step to the side. Don't walk more than two side-by-side.

4 Weather is Erratic

Summers swelter, winters freeze and aside from one magical week in spring and autumn that happens to be perfect, weather here is often temperamental. Pack accordingly.

5 Support Street Performers

'Buskers' are like the subway's court musicians, serenading riders with string concertos, barbershop quartets and bucket-drum percussion. Over 350 acts belong to Music Under New York, a performing arts program administered by the Metropolitan Transit Authority (MTA). Many others strike out independently, and plenty bring music to spaces like Washington Square Park. If you like what you hear, drop them a dollar.

6 It's a Jungle Out There

A surprising amount of wildlife adapts to urban living. Many are rare: a coyote sighting in Central Park or a humpback whale breaching in New York Harbor. Others are more common, like red-tailed hawks hunting for squirrels and painted turtles sunning on pond rocks and ducks – which you might see in Central Park or the East River. None, however, come close in numbers to the squadrons of pigeons and armies of rats that rule the skies and streets.

In 2023 the city hired its first-ever Rat Czar to mitigate the rodent population – which numbered three million at the time. There's even a Rat Academy – a pest control class taught by the city's health department. Extinguishing the critters won't be a walk in the park. NYC's aging infrastructure, paired with a booming population and abundance of tasty trash, are the ideal ingredients for a rat-tastic buffet. Expect to see tailed terrors – especially at night.

7 Reserve Your Spot

New Yorkers are ruthless when it comes to booking seats for popular Broadway shows, tables at trendy restaurants and tickets to limited-run art exhibits. If you want to join the in-crowd, plan ahead. Start booking theater as soon as possible, high-end restaurants one month in advance and museum shows roughly one week prior.

Read, Listen, Watch & Follow

READ

The Age of Innocence (Edith Wharton; 1920) Portrait of Gilded Age scandal among NYC socialites – and a 1993 Scorsese film.

Down These Mean Streets (Piri Thomas; 1967) A bildungsroman chronicling tough times in Spanish Harlem.

Just Kids (Patti Smith; 2010) A real-life snapshot of Smith and Robert Mapplethorpe in '60s and '70s Manhattan.

Vanishing New York (Jeremiah Moss; 2017) Emotional nonfiction exploring socioeconomic forces of NYC gentrification.

LISTEN

Bowery Boys (Greg Young & Tom Meyers; 2007–present) Pithy history podcast deep-diving down NYC's back alleys.

Rhapsody in Blue (George Gershwin, Paul Whiteman Concert Orchestra; 1924) The first recording of Brooklyn-born Gershwin's sonic portrait of NYC.

Marquee Moon (Television; 1977) One of CBGB's breakout bands evokes bohemian East Village adventures with post-punk power chords.

Ready to Die (The Notorious B.I.G; 1994) Brooklyn's favorite son spits autobiographical poetry about a violent upbringing in Kings County.

Hamilton
(Lin Manuel Miranda; 2015) America's Founding Fathers tell historic NYC tales through the hip-hoppified lens of musical theater.

WATCH

The Apartment (1960) An insurance clerk offers his Upper West Side apartment as a pad for philandering higher-ups.

The Muppets Take Manhattan (1984) Jim Henson's zany anthropomorphized animals try to make it on Broadway (pictured top right).

Do the Right Thing (1989) Spike Lee's dramedy probes racial tensions bubbling beneath Brooklyn's surface.

Paris Is Burning (1990) A dazzling, intimate documentary about NYC's underground drag ball scene in the 1980s.

Angels in America (2003) Mike Nichols' movie version of Tony Kushner's stage play recalling the AIDS crisis in Manhattan (pictured bottom right).

AJ PICS / ALAMY STOCK PHOTO ©

PICTORIAL PRESS LTD/ALAMY STOCK PHOTO ©

FOLLOW

@got2gonyc
Videos and reviews of NYC's best and worst public restrooms.

@humansofny
Photoblog with thousands of interviews of standout New Yorkers.

@nyctourism
Guides featuring the latest things to do around town.

New York Magazine
(nymag.com) Dishy news stories chronicling all-things NYC and beyond.

The Infatuation
(theinfatuation.com) Great places to eat around town.

LOWER MANHATTAN & NEW YORK HARBOR

ARCHITECTURE | HERITAGE | WATERFRONT

LOWER MANHATTAN & NEW YORK HARBOR
Trip Builder

TAKE YOUR PICK OF MUST-SEES AND HIDDEN GEMS

Business first: Lower Manhattan encompasses the Financial District (FiDi) and Tribeca. Pleasure second: this is where to spot city icons like the Statue of Liberty and One World Trade Center. Navigate FiDi's skyscraper canyons, skip between trendy Tribeca's shops and bistros then sail offshore to harbor islands, overlooking the urban forestry from afar.

Neighborhood Notes

Best for Architectural delights and waterfront leisure.

Transportation The A/C, J/Z, 2/3 and 4/5 serve main hub Fulton St; the 1 serves South Ferry.

Getting around Explore on foot, or bike the perimeter.

Tip For a free cruise through New York Harbor, hop on the Staten Island Ferry.

FROM LEFT: FELIX MIZIOZNIKOV/SHUTTERSTOCK ©, ANNE CZICHOS/SHUTTERSTOCK ©, PREVIOUS SPREAD: NITO/SHUTTERSTOCK ©

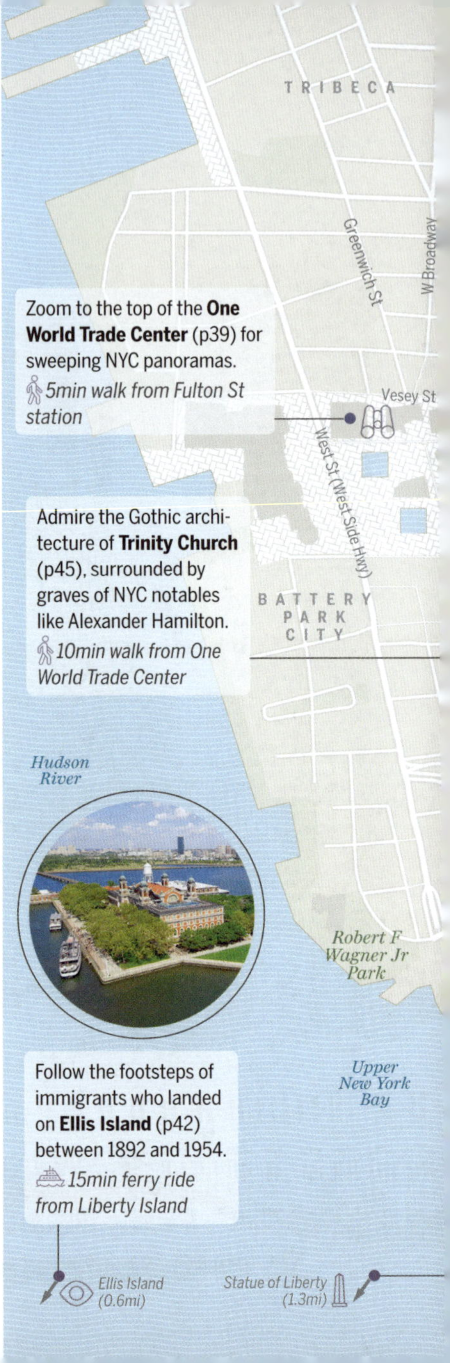
TRIBECA
Greenwich St
W Broadway
Vesey St
West St (West Side Hwy)
BATTERY PARK CITY
Hudson River
Robert F Wagner Jr Park
Upper New York Bay
Ellis Island (0.6mi)
Statue of Liberty (1.3mi)

Zoom to the top of the **One World Trade Center** (p39) for sweeping NYC panoramas.
5min walk from Fulton St station

Admire the Gothic architecture of **Trinity Church** (p45), surrounded by graves of NYC notables like Alexander Hamilton.
10min walk from One World Trade Center

Follow the footsteps of immigrants who landed on **Ellis Island** (p42) between 1892 and 1954.
15min ferry ride from Liberty Island

0 500 m
0 0.25 miles

CHINATOWN

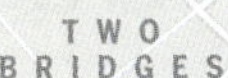

Chambers St
Warren St
City Hall Park
Broadway
Church St
Park Row
LOWER MANHATTAN
Fulton St
Pearl St
Brooklyn Bridge

Learn about NYC's nautical history before boarding the historic ships at **South Street Seaport Museum** (p40).
2min walk from Pier 17

SOUTH STREET SEAPORT

Graze around the **Tin Building** (p41) before catching a Pier 17 concert with Brooklyn Bridge views.
15min walk from Fulton St station

Step inside the **National Museum of the American Indian** (p45) to glimpse beaux arts details and examine Indigenous stories.
1min walk from the Battery

East River
Franklin D Roosevelt Dr
Water St
Greenwich St
Broadway
Beaver St
FINANCIAL DISTRICT
Battery Pl
Whitehall St

Clink glasses at **Fraunces Tavern** (p39), once frequented by America's Founding Fathers.
5min walk from the Battery

Battery Park

Skip around the waterfront **Battery Park** (p39), home to the spectacular SeaGlass Carousel and scores of monuments.
1min walk from South Ferry station

Wave to the beguiling green **Statue of Liberty** (p42), standing guard in New York Harbor.
15min ferry from the Battery (near Castle Clinton)

Governors Island (0.25mi)

Cycle or stroll around car-free **Governors Island** (p36), sprinkled with food trucks, hammocks and a spa.
5min ferry from the Battery Maritime Building

01 SAIL TO Governors Island

RECREATION | RELAXATION | VIEWS

Car-free, glamp-ready and laced with paths for strolling and cycling: Governors Island might be just a five-minute ferry ride from Manhattan's southern tip, but it's energetically worlds away. This military fortress-turned-maritime park is New York Harbor's recreational darling thanks to 172 ice-cream-cone-shaped acres sprinkled with activities to please all palates.

YMGERMAN/SHUTTERSTOCK ©

How to

Getting here Ferries depart from Lower Manhattan's Battery Maritime Building daily. Adult tickets cost $4; on weekends, passengers ride free until noon.

When to go Most outdoor food options open on summer weekends. Winter is a fantastic time to unwind in QC NY's spa.

Seasonal events Visiting in June or August? Dress up for the biannual **Jazz Age Lawn Party**. jazzagelawnparty.com

Lunch time Reserve a grill at Picnic Point ($26) and fire up food with Lady Liberty views. govisland.com

KROPIC1/SHUTTERSTOCK ©

Top left Governors Island |**Bottom left** Castle Williams

DIY Adventure

Choose your adventure Step off the ferry on a sunny afternoon and the island is your oyster. Art enthusiasts can admire outdoor sculptures, like the indigenous fruit trees populating *Open Orchard* – a living earthwork. Kids get thrills zooming down the city's longest slide, a 57ft screamer found on the aptly named **Slide Hill**. If you want to catch rays, head to **Hammock Grove** and rock in one of the area's 50 latticed swings. When hunger calls, skip to an alfresco waterfront restaurant overlooking Lower Manhattan: bite into Baja flavors at **Taco Vista** or slurp down briny bivalves at **Island Oyster**.

Relax in luxury Drop some dough and this people's park becomes an elegant getaway. The Roman-style spa (starting at $98) at **QC NY SPA** has a series of saunas, steam rooms and a heated infinity pool ideal for soaking up city views. Too relaxed for the trip back to Manhattan? Throw a slumber party inside a seasonal glamping tent by **Collective Retreats** (from $215 per night, April to November).

Bike the perimeter Walking through this public park is excellent, but biking is an easier way to fit in all the sights. Cyclists can pedal around 7 miles of trails for panoramas of Lower Manhattan's skyline, the Verrazzano-Narrows Bridge and a Lady Liberty close-up. Rent wheels from **Blazing Saddles** ($30 per day) or use one of several Citi Bike stations around the island.

Island Under Construction

Governors Island has seen tremendous transformations since the indigenous Lenape fished here in the 1500s and called it Paggank, or 'Nut Island'. It's now 100 acres larger, bulked up in 1912 with debris from the Lexington Ave subway excavation and decorated with architectural remnants from its two centuries as a military stronghold. **Fort Jay** and **Castle Williams**, completed in the early 19th century, are the most impressive structures, both of which served as prisons for Confederate soldiers during the Civil War. You can wander the grounds on self-guided tours (10am to 5pm Wednesday to Sunday). The island's newest addition is slated for a 2028 arrival – a Stony Brook University campus dedicated to researching climate change solutions.

02 Underground HISTORY

ARCHITECTURE | MONUMENTS | LEGACY

New York's shimmering skyscrapers beg pedestrians to gaze upward, but if your head is in the clouds, you'll miss the history underfoot. In Lower Manhattan, a trove of yesteryear surprises hide underneath centuries of cement. Colonial skeletons lurk below sidewalks, indigenous trails run beneath the road and sunken memorials honor the city's most recent scars.

HEMIS/ALAMY STOCK PHOTO ©

How to

Getting around Take the 4/5/6 to Bowling Green; start at the Netherland Monument at Battery Pl and State St. Expect to cover roughly 1 mile.

When to go Visit during business hours.

Subterranean tombstones For more underground history, visit the **African Burial Ground National Monument**, where over 15,000 African souls were interred between the 17th and 18th centuries. Archaeologists unearthed the site in 1991.

MARIUSZ LOPUSIEWICZ/SHUTTERSTOCK ©

Indigenous origins Start at the **Battery** – a waterfront park built atop a 19th-century landfill. Before the Dutch dubbed it New Amsterdam and the British renamed it New York, indigenous Lenape communities hunted and fished along the shores of what they called Manahatta. Ponder the Financial District's first shady business transaction at the park's **Netherland Monument**. The statue recalls Dutch merchant Peter Minuit's 'purchase' of the island from the Lenape in 1626. His offering? Some small trinkets.

Founding Fathers Refuel at **Fraunces Tavern** (11.30am-1am), which opened as a saloon in 1762 and now serves as a restaurant and mini museum. In 1783 George Washington bid his officers farewell in the 2nd-floor parlor after winning the American Revolution. Across the street, look for the bones of **Lovelace Tavern's** foundation buried beneath the sidewalk. Built in 1670 and burned down in 1706, the site wasn't rediscovered until 1979.

Fallen heroes Walk along **Wall St** (an actual defense wall in the 17th century, marking New Amsterdam's edge) then head north on **Broadway** (a roadway following a Lenape trading route called the Wickquasgeck Trail) and you'll eventually see One World Trade Center gleaming westward. Below the tower, two pools cascading 30ft into a dark void memorialize those lost in the 1983 World Trade Center car bombing and September 11 – the deadliest attack on US soil and New York's darkest day.

Top left Netherland Monument, the Battery **Bottom left** Fraunces Tavern

NYC From Above

After taking in history from below, wow over views of **One World Trade Center** (aka Freedom Tower; onewtc.com; 9am-9pm). The shimmering glass spectacle soars 1776ft into the air like a phoenix – a testament to NYC's post-September 11 rebirth. The building is impressive from ground level, but wait until you reach **One World Observatory** (floors 100-102, oneworldobservatory.com). Floor-to-ceiling windows showcase a 360-degree panorama with arresting perspectives of all five boroughs and three adjoining states. If you need help naming landmarks, interactive mobile tablets programmed in multiple languages are available, included in a combo ticket for a well-spent $10 extra.

03 South Street **SEAPORT**

SHOPPING | DINING | PRESERVATION

Manhattan's historic trading port has come a long way since Hurricane Sandy flooded its cobblestone streets in 2012. In the storm's aftermath, real-estate developers swooped in and transformed these 4 acres into the center of Lower Manhattan's urban renaissance. Today, food markets, boutiques and a maritime museum tempt visitors. Spend a few hours soaking it all in.

RBLFMR/SHUTTERSTOCK ©

How to

Getting here Take the A/C, 2/3, J/Z or 4/5 train to Fulton St and head toward the East River.

When to go The seaport is most lively on summer weekends, though you'll have to contend with crowds.

Rooftop concerts From May to October, the **Rooftop at Pier 17** (therooftopatpier17.com) presents outdoor concerts with Brooklyn Bridge views. No ticket? No worries: admire the steel suspension stunner from the north side of Pier 17's ground level.

C. TAYLOR CROTHERS/GETTY IMAGES ©

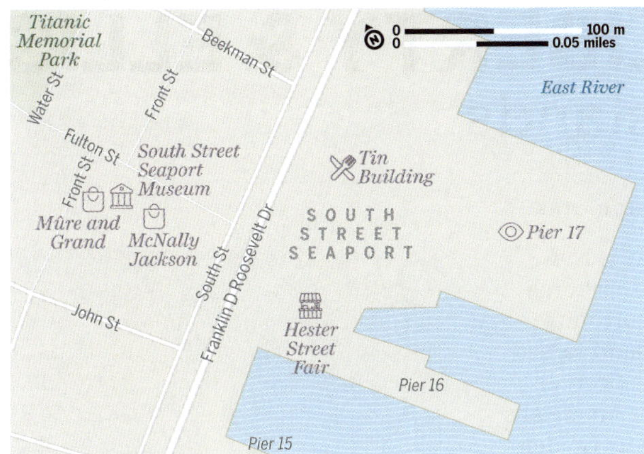

Seaport Itinerary

Sea-faring stories Begin by brushing up on Manhattan's maritime beginnings at the **South Street Seaport Museum**. This area was home to the city's principal port until the Civil War, and its streets still showcase 18th- and 19th-century architecture from its heyday. The museum also cares for a fleet of historic ships that set sail in New York Harbor: a sunset cruise aboard the 1885 schooner **Pioneer** is particularly romantic (adult child $70/30).

Modern markets You won't find the seaport's fish market and brothels of yore, but modern merchants here sell top-grade goods. New York bookstore chain **McNally Jackson** is a word-nerd wonderland and the flower-power threads at **Mûre and Grand** are a ray of sunshine. It's worth scheduling a trip around the **Hester Street Fair** (hesterstreetfair.com), Pier 17's summer weekend pop-up, where vendors sell vintage thrift clothes, handmade jewelry and other uber-cool knickknacks.

Sips and snacks Break up the shopping by imbibing at bars along the piers. In the **Tin Building**, a 53,000-sq-ft food emporium by restaurateur Jean-George Vongerichten, it's possible to hop around specialty counters for wine, beer and cocktails. At Pier 17's **Pearl Alley** (the restaurant, not the street), you can grab a negroni while gawking at views of Brooklyn. There's also no shortage of fabulous food, with **Carne Mare** (Italian chophouse) and **House of the Red Pearl** (upscale Chinese) topping the list.

Top left South Street Seaport
Bottom left Pier 17

Pearl St's Briny Past

There are several theories concerning the origin of Pearl St's name – all revolving around oysters. The most popular says the street was paved with their pearl-white shells – a cheap building material, considering thick beds of the decadent aphrodisiacs once lined the city's estuaries. After Europeans arrived, NYC earned a reputation as the world's oyster capital; some biologists estimate New York Harbor contained half the globe's supply. But by 1927, pollution and overharvesting killed masses of mollusks. Today NYC is dedicated to repopulating these natural filtration systems. The **Billion Oyster Project** hopes to add one billion briny bivalves to the local ecosystem by 2035.

04 LIBERTY & ELLIS Islands

LANDMARKS | SAILING | PANORAMAS

The Statue of Liberty is New York's most enduring icon, her torch shining as a beacon of opportunity since 1886. Nearby Ellis Island served as America's immigration epicenter from 1892 to 1924 – 40% of Americans can trace their ancestry to its Golden Door. Visit both on a scenic New York Harbor ferry ride and learn how NYC became an international melting pot.

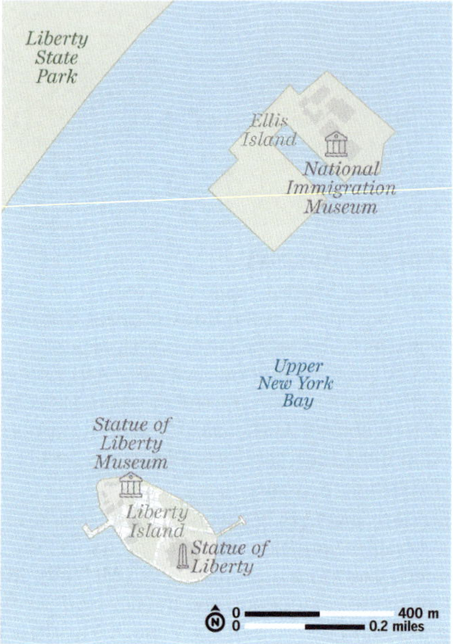

How to

Getting there The 15-minute ferry ride to Liberty Island sets sail from the Battery. Expect airport-style security screenings and 30- to 90-minute lines during summer's high season. All ferries stop at Ellis Island before returning to Manhattan.

When to go To see both Liberty and Ellis Island on the same day, hop on a ferry before 2pm.

Tickets Statue City Cruises (statuecitycruises.com) is the only ferry service that sails to Liberty and Ellis Islands. Book tickets in advance.

Harbor History

Learn about the statue Step into Liberty Island's free **museum** for a riveting introduction to the 'Lady'. The statue's original torch, removed in 1984, is the visual pièce de résistance, while the most engaging exhibit digs into the statue's hypocrisy. In 1886, 'universal liberty' was a dream deferred for many Americans: women didn't have the right to vote and African Americans suffered through racist government policies during post-Civil War Reconstruction.

Arrive at Ellis Island Traveling to Ellis Island begins as it did for roughly 12 million immigrants – on the water. The 27.5-acre plot of land is only accessible via ferry, which leaves from Liberty Island before sailing another

Top right Statue of Liberty
Bottom right National Immigration Museum

ANDREY DENISYUK/GETTY IMAGES ©

ZACK FRANK/SHUTTERSTOCK ©

The Goddess

Designer Frédéric-Auguste Bartholdi's 450,000-pound Statue of Liberty was constructed in Paris between 1881 and 1884 with help from French engineer Alexandre Gustave Eiffel (of the eponymous tower) using 300 copper sheets, each about 7.8ft wide. She was transported to New York across the treacherous Atlantic then placed on a granite pedestal designed by architect Richard Morris Hunt, bringing her total height to 305ft. Her green 'patina'? The result of oxidized copper.

15 minutes to the **National Immigration Museum**.

Understand the US Immerse yourself in the complex tapestry of US immigration around the 1st-floor museum of Ellis Island's **Main Building**. *Journeys: The Peopling of America, 1550–1890* traces the movement of people to and through the US.

Follow immigrant footsteps On the 2nd floor, walk *Through America's Gate* – an exhibition chronicling the harrowing step-by-step process for newly arrived immigrants. Officials blocked roughly 2% of people from entry to the US – usually due to disease, disability or the perceived inability to support themselves – sometimes accounting for over 1000 travelers per month.

Listings

BEST OF THE REST

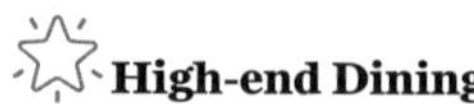

High-end Dining

Manhatta $$$

Splurge on the tasting menu (10 courses, $275) or sip a $20-plus cocktail bar-side. The high prices pay for what's important – sweeping views from the 60th floor.

Frenchette $$$

Frequented by Tribeca's trendy set, this contemporary French bistro is more Left Bank Paris than West Side Manhattan. The 'amuse' portion of the menu (small plates) satisfies even the pickiest 'bouche.'

Tiny's & the Bar Upstairs $$$

Dine on modern American plates with French accents inside this blushing pink townhouse from 1810, decorated with salvaged wood paneling and original tin ceilings.

Odeon $$$

The red neon sign glowing above this bistro since 1980 is almost as storied as the restaurant itself, once frequented by tastemakers like Warhol and Scorsese. Brunch remains top tier.

Cheap Eats & Comfort Food

Leo's Bagels $

Hand-rolled gluten heaven: expect lightly crisped bottoms and chewy interiors, perfect with a simple cream cheese schmear or possibly topped with lox (smoked salmon).

Pearl Diner $

Skyscrapers might've redrawn the neighborhood, but this unfussy, old-school, swivel-stool classic remains seemingly unchanged, serving fluffy pancakes and an array of burgers since the 1960s.

Pisillo $

Tiny shop near the Brooklyn Bridge with super-big Italian sandwiches. Eat yours on a bench in City Hall Park or jockey for seats alongside FiDi's worker bees.

Brookfield Place $$

Wander two fancy food courts at this retail space across from One World Trade Center: **Le District**, a gourmet Francophile foodie marketplace, and **Hudson Eats**, a mess hall with popular chain quick bites.

Dynamo Drinks

Overstory $$$

This lofty lounge on the 64th floor is best for marveling at the city's sparkling lights. Reserve an outdoor table ($75 minimum); order a cocktail and light bites.

Dead Rabbit $$

It's tough beating this three-floor bar named after a feared 19th-century Irish-American gang. You'll find no gangs here today, but the Irish coffee (hot or frozen) is a knockout.

Smith & Mills $$$

Head to the Tribeca location of this cocktail bar and restaurant, housed in a former carriage house. Don't leave without peeping into the bathroom – it's a 1902 cage elevator.

Singular Shops

CityStore

Buy exclusive, city-licensed merchandise like authentic-looking taxi medallions, subway signs, FDNY shirts and normcore tees repping your favorite borough. Located inside the grand Manhattan Municipal Building.

Mysterious Bookshop

Bibliophiles come to this mystery-themed paperback palace, open since 1979, to sleuth for titles relating to crime, espionage and anything else inciting suspense.

Philip Williams Posters

Leaf through this block-long room's collection of 10,000 printed pieces, separated into stacks with everything from vintage *New Yorker* covers to 19th-century advertisements on canvas.

Magnificent Architecture

Woolworth Building

The world's tallest building from 1913 to 1930, Cass Gilbert's 792ft-tall masterpiece is a neo-Gothic marvel clad in masonry and terra-cotta.

St Paul's Chapel

Manhattan's oldest-standing church, the 'little chapel that stood,' has survived everything since 1766 – including the day the Twin Towers crumbled less than 100yd away in 2001.

Trinity Church

Come to this church – staring down Wall St since 1846 – to check out the three sets of bronze doors designed by Richard Morris Hunt, elaborate stained-glass windows and Alexander Hamilton's grave. www.trinitywallstreet.org

Oculus

Santiago Calatrava's gleaming cream dove (or intergalactic spaceship, depending on who you talk to) perches above the World Trade Center's mall-and-transit hub with 36,500 tons of steel.

Outdoor Sculptures & Sights

Fearless Girl

Standing 4ft tall, Kristen Visbal's bronze sculpture defiantly holds her ground before

ASTUDIO/SHUTTERSTOCK ©

Oculus

the New York Stock Exchange (NYSE) near Wall St – encouraging gender diversity in a male-dominated workplace.

Charging Bull

Bowling Green's 7000-pound animal, installed in 1989 as a piece of guerrilla art by sculptor Arturo Di Modica, supposedly brings financial prosperity – as long as you rub its bronze testicles.

SeaGlass Carousel

Battery Park visitors sit atop iridescent, fiberglass fish to spin around a swirling glass-and-steel pavilion. Lights mimic an underwater wonderland. seaglasscarousel.nyc

Free Museums

National Museum of the American Indian

Exhibits explore indigenous life, from ancient to contemporary times, inside Cass Gilbert's 1907 Customs House – a beaux-arts beauty with a 140-ton skylight serving as the interior's showpiece. www.nmai.si.edu

Federal Hall

A bronze statue of George Washington stands above Wall St on the steps of this Greek Revival eye-catcher, sitting atop the place where he was sworn in as President in 1789.

SOHO, NOLITA, CHINATOWN & LITTLE ITALY

ARTISTIC | INTERNATIONAL | UPSCALE

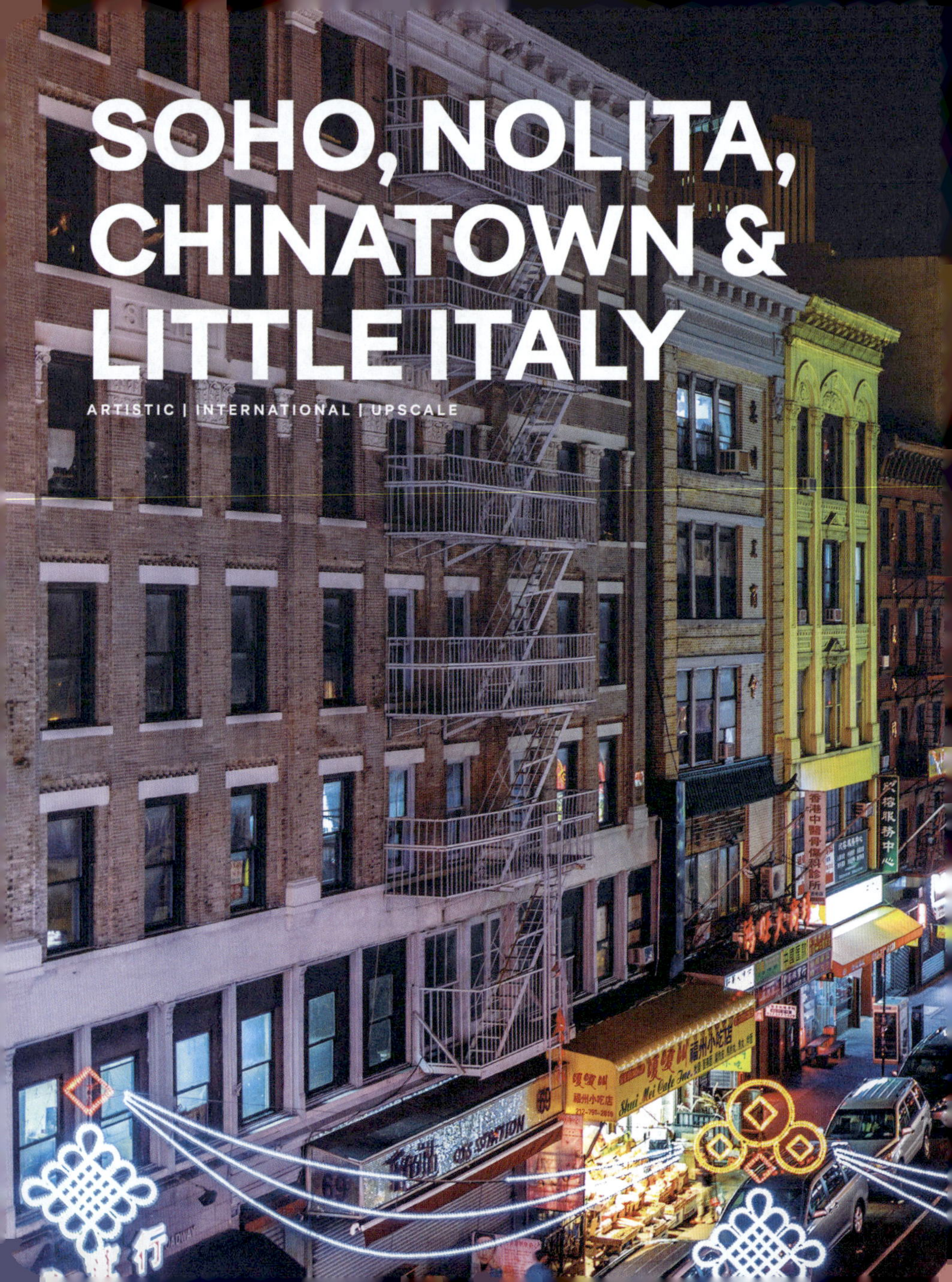

60號怡豐商場

SOHO, NOLITA, CHINATOWN & LITTLE ITALY Trip Builder

TAKE YOUR PICK OF MUST-SEES AND HIDDEN GEMS

SoHo (South of Houston) and Nolita (North of Little Italy) dominate as Manhattan's trendsetting epicenters, home to boutiques, bars and eateries that appear to pop from the pages of *Vogue*. Chinatown and Little Italy simmer with the nostalgia of far-off homelands, tasted in distinctive cuisines served along their streets.

Neighborhood Notes

Best for Shopping, gallery hopping and international restaurants.

Getting around Canal St is the main artery separating SoHo and Chinatown, serviced east to west by the J/Z, 6, N/Q/R, A/C/E and 1 trains.

Top tip Traffic gets congested around here – avoid cabs and buses.

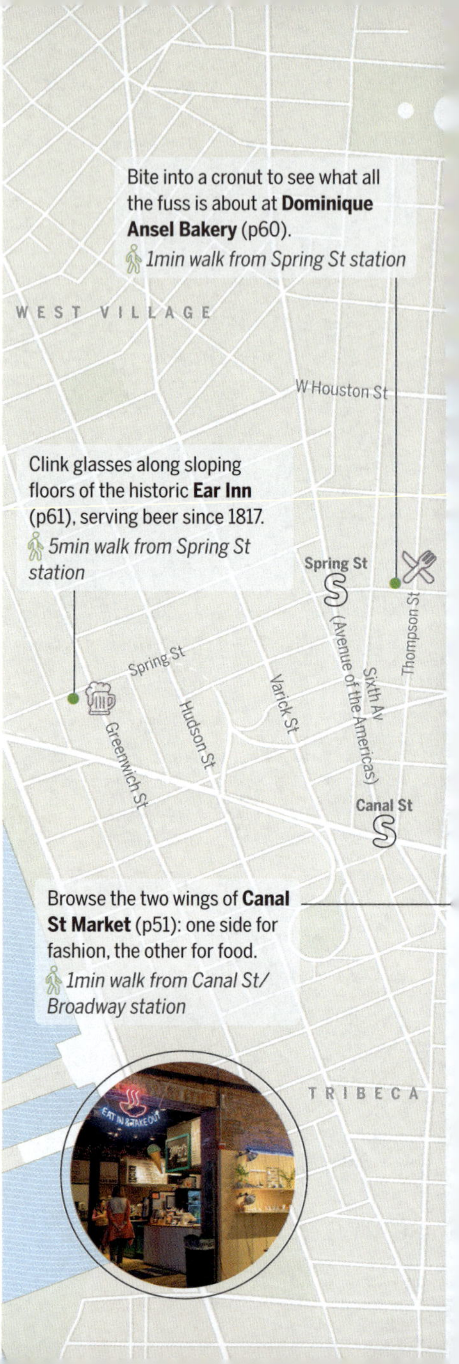
Bite into a cronut to see what all the fuss is about at **Dominique Ansel Bakery** (p60).
1min walk from Spring St station
WEST VILLAGE
W Houston St
Clink glasses along sloping floors of the historic **Ear Inn** (p61), serving beer since 1817.
5min walk from Spring St station
Spring St
Thompson St
Spring St
Varick St
(Avenue of the Americas)
Sixth Av
Hudson St
Greenwich St
Canal St
Browse the two wings of **Canal St Market** (p51): one side for fashion, the other for food.
1min walk from Canal St/ Broadway station
TRIBECA
EAT IN & TAKE OUT

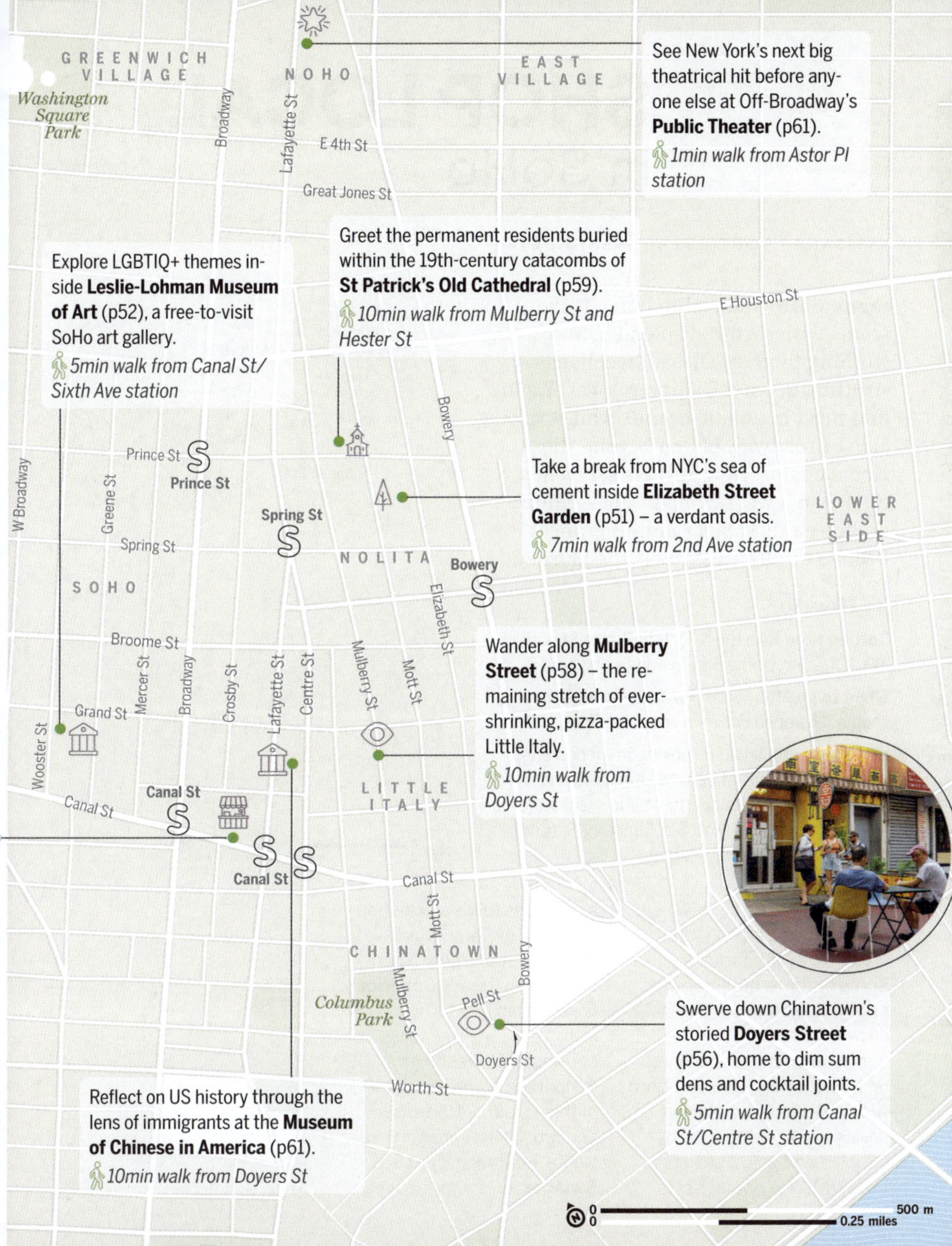

See New York's next big theatrical hit before anyone else at Off-Broadway's **Public Theater** (p61).
1min walk from Astor Pl station
Greet the permanent residents buried within the 19th-century catacombs of **St Patrick's Old Cathedral** (p59).
10min walk from Mulberry St and Hester St
Explore LGBTIQ+ themes inside **Leslie-Lohman Museum of Art** (p52), a free-to-visit SoHo art gallery.
5min walk from Canal St/Sixth Ave station
Take a break from NYC's sea of cement inside **Elizabeth Street Garden** (p51) – a verdant oasis.
7min walk from 2nd Ave station
Wander along **Mulberry Street** (p58) – the remaining stretch of ever-shrinking, pizza-packed Little Italy.
10min walk from Doyers St
Swerve down Chinatown's storied **Doyers Street** (p56), home to dim sum dens and cocktail joints.
5min walk from Canal St/Centre St station
Reflect on US history through the lens of immigrants at the **Museum of Chinese in America** (p61).
10min walk from Doyers St
GREENWICH VILLAGE
Washington Square Park
NOHO
EAST VILLAGE
Broadway
Lafayette St
E 4th St
Great Jones St
E Houston St
Bowery
Prince St
Prince St
W Broadway
Greene St
Spring St
Spring St
NOLITA
Bowery
LOWER EAST SIDE
SOHO
Elizabeth St
Broome St
Mercer St
Broadway
Crosby St
Lafayette St
Centre St
Mulberry St
Mott St
Grand St
Wooster St
LITTLE ITALY
Canal St
Canal St
Canal St
Canal St
Mott St
CHINATOWN
Bowery
Columbus Park
Mulberry St
Pell St
Doyers St
Worth St
0 500 m
0 0.25 miles

05 SHOP LOCAL in SoHo

ARTISANS | BOUTIQUES | FASHIONISTAS

SoHo and Nolita burst at the seams with sartorial splendor, and strolling their streets can feel like strutting down a fashion runway. You'll find most big-name brands while cruising along Broadway, but go beyond those global chains. New Yorkers set trends thanks to jewel-box boutiques selling unique clothes, kicks and fragrances. Browse or buy – the joy is the journey.

How to

Getting here Take the N/Q/R to Prince St at the heart of SoHo, or the 6 to Spring St and hoof it.

When to go Afternoons are best – nearly every shop will be open between noon and 5pm.

Stylish streets If you're looking to window shop, venture down Mott St between Kenmare and E Houston. A bouquet of perfume and scent stores adorn Elizabeth and Mott Sts. Mulberry St (Little Italy's heart) is equally alluring.

Local designers For a sense of local style, stop in stores created by New Yorkers. Some of these boutiques get pricey, but it's worth perusing each showroom – they're like mini fashion museums. First up is jewelry by Brooklyn-born **Alexis Bittar**, who started selling his signature Lucite baubles on SoHo's streets in the 1980s. He now attracts glamazons to his sleek shop designed by Tony Award–winning set designer Scott Pask. Then there's **Corridor**'s creator Dan Snyder, who went from being an FBI intelligence contractor in Washington, DC, to hocking his menswear line of thick plaid button-downs and crocheted cardigans in Nolita. Rounding it out is **R Swiader** – New York-based

Top right Elizabeth Street Garden
Bottom right Shoppers in SoHo

POPOVA VALERIYA/SHUTTERSTOCK ©

A Garden Break

If the slender stores start feeling claustrophobic, catch your breath at **Elizabeth Street Garden** – a hidden oasis between Prince and Spring Sts. It began in 1991 when an antiques dealer leased the abandoned lot from the city, added landscaping and sprinkled the acre with sculptures. This whimsical spot is now a serene refuge for shop-weary New Yorkers. Grab a cup of Nicaraguan coffee from **Cafe Integral**, a short walk away, to enjoy amid the flora.

designer Raf Swiader's home for gender-optional clothing, which shirks conventions by doubling as a salon.

Browse the markets For thriftier threads and on-the-rise artisans, wander **Canal St Market** – a food hall and retail hub with vintage wares, K-pop clothes and jewelry. For fantastic street vendors, skip to **Nolita Market** (on Prince St between Mulberry and Mott) – a block lined with handmade trinkets and art.

Stores with stay power Leather store **Schott** started selling coats in 1913; everyone from Marlon Brando to the Ramones has sported their jackets. **Wing On Wo & Co**, founded in the 1890s, is Chinatown's oldest continually operating store, packed with porcelain treasures like kitchen accessories and jewelry.

RBLFMR/ SHUTTERSTOCK ©

06 See SoHo's ART SCENE

GALLERIES | MINIMALISM | SIDEWALK ART

Fashionistas lust over SoHo's flagship stores today, but in the 1960s many New Yorkers considered the area a wasteland – unless they were among the artists living in its industrial loft spaces. By the 1980s, these creative crowds turned SoHo into NYC's arty epicenter. Look beyond the storefronts to eye the neighborhood's stylish origins.

Trip Notes

Getting here/around Take the A/C/E to Canal, then head north on Wooster St. Walking between all five destinations covers ¾ of a mile.

When to go Visit between Wednesday and Saturday, when all destinations are open. Check hours before showing up – most open from noon to 6pm.

Save a buck All of these galleries are free to visit. Use your savings to grab coffee at **NowHere**, a gallery space and cafe.

Artsy Real Estate

The cheap housing stock that attracted artists to SoHo is gone – but you can still glimpse how the creative kind once lived. Join a guided tour of minimalist maverick Donald Judd's former **SoHo home** and studio. He purchased the five-story cast-iron building in 1968 for a now unthinkable $68,000. juddfoundation.org

05 Watch out for **Ken Hiratsuka's sidewalk carving** outside of Prada – one of 40 he sculpted after moving to NYC in 1982.

04 Buzz the 2nd floor of 141 Wooster St to see the **New York Earth Room**, filled with 280,000lb of dirt since 1980.

03 Contemplate each pencil stroke at the **Drawing Center** (pictured left), a nonprofit focused solely on drawings since its opening in 1977.

02 Browse LGBTIQ+-focused **Leslie-Lohman Museum of Art**, whose groundbreaking founders began showcasing gay creations from a SoHo loft in 1969.

01 Admire avant-garde art at the **Jeffrey Deitch Gallery**, founded by Deitch, a fixture of New York's art scene since the 1970s.

TASTE THE FLAVORS
of Chinatown

01 Dr Clark's
Order sushi and *jingi-sukan* (Ghengis Khan–inspired BBQ lamb, cooked table-side) at this restaurant serving Hokkaido cuisine.

02 Fried Dumpling
Hole-in-the-wall counter for dumplings: order 13 for $5, arguably one of the cheapest ways to get your fill in Manhattan.

03 Peking Duck House
If you're in the mood for crispy duck, this is the place. Don't forget to BYOB (bring your own booze).

04 Original Chinatown Ice Cream Factory
This isn't your standard ice-cream shop. Taste test a wide variety of flavors, from black sesame to lychee to red bean.

05 Mei Li Wah
It's worth waiting in line for a shiny pineapple bun – either savory (roasted pork) or sweet (custard).

06 Tasty Hand-Pulled Noodles
Savor a greasy bowl of hot-to-go pan-fried noodles on Doyers St.

07 Golden Diner
Eat American diner classics with Asian flavors,

like the chicken-katsu club or anything sweetened with yuzu.

08 Hop Kee

Dive into the basement for your fill of Cantonese-style snails, crabs and broccoli in oyster sauce.

09 Jing Fong Restaurant

Gather a group for dim sum at this restaurant, where carts of favorites like fried turnip cakes roll past packed tables.

10 Pinklady Cheese Tart

Get a painter's palette of fluffy Japanese baked-cheese tarts in flavors like matcha, ube and chocolate.

11 Fu Zhou Wei Zhong Wei Jia Xiang Feng Wei

Look past East Broadway Mall's grungy vestibules and head downstairs for steamed buns at 'the tastiest Fuzhou hometown-flavor restaurant.'

12 Veggie dim sum at Buddha Bodai

Chinatown's unfussy go-to for vegetarian and certified kosher cuisine, serving classic Cantonese flavors. Dim sum is served until 4pm; BYOB.

07 Doyers Street's DARK SIDE

DINING | DRINKING | CULTURE

In a city dominated by a regimented grid, this curved block at Chinatown's heart refuses to conform. Wander the 200ft-long outlier, which has transformed from a meandering stream to America's deadliest block to a pedestrian-only playground serving Asian-inspired food and drinks. Whether you spend half an hour or an evening here, Doyers introduces this immigrant neighborhood's idiosyncrasies.

FLEQUILU/SHUTTERSTOCK ©

How to

Getting here Take the N/Q/R/W or J/Z to Canal St and weave through Chinatown to Doyers St.

When to go Arrive in the early evening for dinner and cocktails.

People watch Amble through **Columbus Park** on your way from the subway to Doyers St. The leafy space is like a portal to Shanghai, with spirited mah-jongg meisters, slow-motion tai-chi practitioners and locals gossiping over homemade dumplings.

CHOONGKY/SHUTTERSTOCK ©

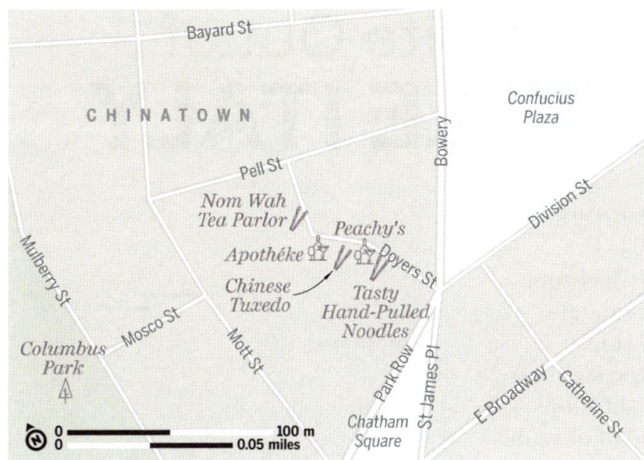

Dim Sum & Craft Cocktails

Long lasting flavor Bite into Doyers' culinary heritage at **Nom Wah Tea Parlor** (11am-9pm) – the oldest dim sum place in town, dating back to the 1920s. Grab a seat at one of the red banquettes or counter stools (outdoor tables are lovely on sunny summer days, though hard to snag) and tick off what you want on the menu provided. Roast pork buns, Shanghainese soup dumplings, shrimp *siu mai* (steamed dumplings) – it's all finger-licking good. If you can't get a table (lines are common), you can still get a taste of Doyers history by dining at **Chinese Tuxedo**, a bi-level fine-dining restaurant that housed the city's first Chinese theater. Still not satiated? Take a few steps to super-cheap, no-frills **Tasty Hand-Pulled Noodles**. The name says it all.

Drinks after dark The opium dens of yore might be gone, but when the sun goes down, Doyers is still Chinatown's best place to let loose. If you dig sipping sake or cocktails next to a picture-perfect neon-pink dragon, head to **Peachy's** (from 6pm Tue-Sat) – a bar underneath the Chinese Tuxedo. **Apothéke** (from 6:30pm Tue-Sun), an apothecary-style mixology lounge a few steps away, gets scientific with spirits in a former opium den. Look for the 'chemist' sign with a beaker illustration above the doorway and grab a seat to watch skilled barkeeps make liquid magic. Keep the visit on theme by ordering a pineapple-lemongrass-infused Sitting Buddha.

Top left Doyers Street
Bottom left Columbus Park

A Deadly History

Named after Hendrick Doyer, an 18th-century Dutch immigrant who owned a distillery here, Doyers became the epicenter of Chinatown as it took shape in the late 1800s. (A careless street-sign painter apparently dropped the apostrophe.) By the end of the century, the street earned new monikers like 'Murder Alley' and the 'Bloody Angle' – references to its criminal activity. Throughout the early 20th century, warring *tongs* (Chinese gangs) attacked rivals by hiding behind the street's sharp bend – a cause for concern among anyone visiting nearby tenement buildings packed with gambling parlors and opium dens. Don't worry: the bloody days are done.

08 Take a Bite Out of LITTLE ITALY

TRADITION | CUISINE | CATACOMBS

New York's Little Italy has gone from 'big boot' to 'ultraslim sandal' over the past 50 years – but skip down Mulberry Street and the sight of gingham tablecloths and pasta shops feels like a portal to the land of olive oil and wine. Eat your way from Italy to Nolita, remembering a time when this whole area was doused in red sauce.

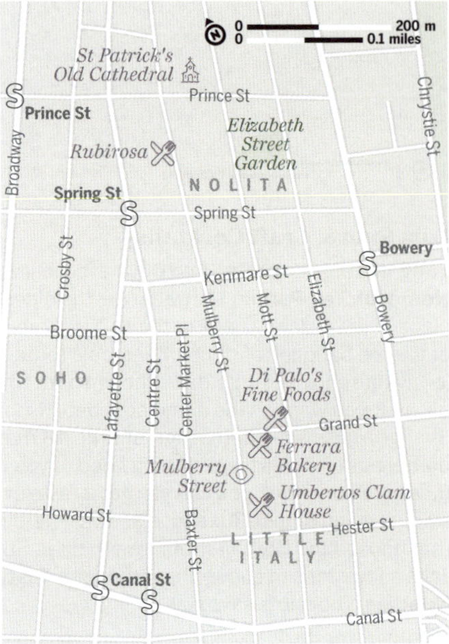

How to

Getting around Begin at the intersection of Hester and Mulberry Sts, where the 'Little Italy' sign soaring above marks Chinatown's encroaching border. Walk north for three blocks to Kenmare St (this is the core of Little Italy) and into Nolita (North of Little Italy).

When to go Visit for an afternoon lunch or early evening dinner.

Street art Check out the **Little Italy Street Art Project** to see murals by big-name artists splashed across the cityscape. lisaprojectnyc.org/murals

Slice of history **Mulberry Street**, named after mulberry trees that once lined its sidewalks, became synonymous with Italy between the 1880s to 1920s as four million Italian immigrants flooded the US. By 1910, roughly 10,000 Italian Americans crammed themselves into a 2-mile radius of tenement buildings; Jacob Riis called it the 'foul core of New York's slums.' But after WWII, the residents decided to say *'arrivederci'* to tenement living, leaving the neighborhood for Brooklyn, the suburbs and beyond.

Taste of the old country Though legions of nonnas abandoned Little Italy's kitchens, there's no shortage of Italian restaurants on Mul-

Top right St Patrick's Old Cathedral
Bottom right Little Italy

JRTWYNAM/SHUTTERSTOCK ©

Cemetery Tour

Continue north on Mulberry St to **St Patrick's Old Cathedral** (not to be confused with Midtown's St Patrick's Cathedral). This Gothic Revival basilica from 1815 was once the seat of religious life for the Archdiocese of New York and a vital community center for Irish Catholic immigrants. Guided tours (takeawalk.com/old-cathedral-tours, $35) wander through the church's catacombs, lit by electric candlelight, to see the final resting place of bishops and notable 19th-century New Yorkers.

berry St. Be discerning: a lot of the food is mediocre. Skip the spiels of restaurant hawkers trying to lure you to their tables and head straight to authentic eateries with staying power. For cheap handheld treats, there's **Ferrara Bakery**, open since 1892 (grab a crisp, sweet ricotta-stuffed cannoli) and **Di Palo's Fine Foods**, which started selling primo cheese over a century ago. Nab a table at **Rubirosa** for pizza perfection: scarf down whisper-thin crust smothered in vodka sauce and mozz. If you're into Little Italy's mob history, grab a seat at **Umbertos Clam House**. In 1972, crime boss Joey Gallo was shot and killed on site. Today, the only thing worth dying for here is the raw oyster bar.

EMIN KULIYEV/SHUTTERSTOCK ©

Listings

BEST OF THE REST

Cronuts & Cakes

Dominique Ansel Bakery $

SoHo's sweet-shop star, thanks to the cronut (a croissant-donut). Also tempting: the buttery *kouign amann* (Breton cake) and the DKA – a caramelized croissant.

Alimama Tea $

Match vegan, gluten-free mochi donuts with cold-brewed tea and cream puffs at this munchkin-sized Bayard St cafe.

Little Cupcake Bakeshop $

This retro bakehouse is famous for its Brooklyn Blackout Cake – a chocolate confection invented by former chain Ebinger's, honoring citywide blackouts to protect the Brooklyn Navy Yard during WWII.

Keki Modern Cakes $

Competition for New York's best cheesecake isn't stiff – it's jiggly. Bounce into this sugar shop for Japanese-style cheesecakes and cream puffs stuffed with flavors like ube and pistachio.

Beloved Bistros

Balthazar $$$

It's been SoHo's French bistro king since 1997 for three reasons: location in NYC's shopping heartland, the uplifting Paris-meets-Manhattan ambiance and the something-for-everyone menu.

Raoul's $$$

Cool kids started lining up for these French bistro classics in 1975. Order the peppercorn-crusted burger with Saint-André cheese – usually the first thing to sell out.

Fanelli Cafe $$

Originally a saloon from 1847, this diner-style cafe is a portal to SoHo's past. Nab the corner table looking down Prince and Mercer Sts to be the envy of TikTok.

Popular Pizza

Prince Street Pizza $

The slightly sweet red sauce, crispy bottom and doughy crust make it worth a slice – particularly if you get pepperoni. But is it worth the long line? Buyer's choice.

Lombardi's $$

This Nolita institution claims to be America's first pizzeria – it started serving delicious Neapolitan-style, coal-fired pies in 1905. Over the past century, word has gotten out: expect crowds.

Asian Flavors

Thai Diner $$

Big Apple goes Bangkok at this tiki temple – think classic NY diner retooled with Southeast Asian flavors. Try the decked-out disco fries and slightly-spicy *baan* salad for dinner; come back for brunch.

Fong On $

Owner Paul Eng carries on his family's legacy at this soy-stocked food counter, initially opened in 1933, serving cups of tofu pudding. Order yours savory, sweet or plain.

Raku $$

The minimalist design lets the important things shine: hot or cold *udon* (thick Japanese noodles), *donburi* (a rice-based dish) and gyoza – all affordable and filling.

Retro Bars

Ear Inn $

See what SoHo was like before the fashionistas took over at this old-guard drinking den in an 18th-century house built for James Brown, George Washington's African American aide.

Spring Lounge $

In Prohibition days, it peddled buckets of beer. In the '60s, its basement was a gambling den. Today it's best known for kooky shark decor and all-night revelry.

Mr Fong's $

This stylish neighborhood bar underneath the rumbling Manhattan Bridge serves Chinese-inspired cocktails, and has its own jukebox.

Cool Cosmetics & Scents

Olfactory NYC

Unlike most perfumeries in Nolita's unofficial fragrance district, this bespoke scent shop allows visitors to craft a signature style with the help of a 'scentologist.'

Atelier Beauté Chanel

Book a small-group makeup happy hour ($55) to sip champagne while picking the perfect shade of lipstick. Shoppers can try products for free before making purchases.

Book Bastions

Housing Works Bookstore

Buy secondhand books, vinyl and comics for a good cause (proceeds go to New York's low-income population affected by HIV and AIDS) or sit in the on-site cafe.

McNally Jackson

Bustling indie MJ's newest location, unveiled in 2023, stocks an excellent selection of magazines and books including fiction, food, architecture, design, history and kids' lit.

Museums, Plays & Music

Museum of Chinese in America

Learn about Chinatown's history through engaging permanent and temporary exhibitions on topics like immigration, cultural identity and racial stereotyping, illuminating the Chinese American experience.

Merchant's House Museum

Tour this red-brick mansion, built in 1832 and purchased by merchant Seabury Treadwell three years later, for an authentic look at 19th-century mercantile life.

Public Theater

This legendary Off-Broadway house, founded in 1954, birthed megawatt musicals like *A Chorus Line* and *Hamilton*. Don't miss adjacent **Joe's Pub** – a bar and cabaret serving top-shelf entertainment.

Fantastic Festivals

Chinatown Night Market

For one Friday every month between May and September, a summer night shindig takes over Forsyth Plaza with local food stands, folksy crafts and dancing in the street. thinkchinatown.org

Feast of San Gennaro

Little Italy's 11-day celebration in September honors the Patron Saint of Naples with a smorgasbord of fried dough, juicy sausages and meatball parms along action-packed Mulberry St.

EAST VILLAGE & THE LOWER EAST SIDE

CULTURED | EDGY | STYLISH

EAST VILLAGE & THE LOWER EAST SIDE
Trip Builder

TAKE YOUR PICK OF MUST-SEES AND HIDDEN GEMS

Generations of immigrants began their American adventure around these side-by-side neighborhoods spiced with multicultural flavor. They are also exceptionally cool. Counterculture kids spent decades finding their bohemian stride down each sidewalk – and though most of the Beatniks, hippies and punk rockers are gone, it remains Manhattan's most eclectic and funky place to be.

Neighborhood Notes

Best for Dining, drinking, avant-garde art and international chutzpah.

Transportation L to First Ave, 6 to Astor Pl, F to Second Ave.

Getting around East Village is north, Lower East Side is south, Houston divides the two.

Stay vigilant Expect seedy vestiges from the punk rock past – part of the charm.

0 500 m
0 0.25 miles
East River
Steam, sauna, cold plunge and repeat with towel-wrapped crowds at the **Russian & Turkish Baths** (p77).
2min walk from Tompkins Square Park
Sit on a bench in **Tompkins Square Park** (p67) and imagine the squatters rioting in 1988.
11min walk from Astor Pl station
Second Ave
First Ave
E 10th St
Tompkins Square Park
St Marks Pl
EAST VILLAGE
Ave B
Ave C
E 7th St
Ave D
Franklin D Roosevelt Dr
Order all the vegetarian sandwiches and sides your stomach can handle at top-notch **Superiority Burger** (p76).
11min walk from Astor Pl station
E 5th St
ALPHABET CITY
East River Park
E 3rd St
E 2nd St
Bite into a pastrami sandwich on rye bread at **Katz's Delicatessen** (p70), a Jewish deli mainstay.
3min walk from Second Ave station
2nd Ave
E Houston St
Essex St
Clinton St
Hamilton Fish Park
Stanton St
Chrystie St
Forsyth St
Rivington St
Delancey-Essex Sts
Witness cramped living quarters of turn-of-the-20th-century immigrants at the **Tenement Museum** (p70).
3min walk from Delancey St/Essex St station
Williamsburg Bridge
Sara D Roosevelt Park
Delancey St
Bowery
Broome St
LOWER EAST SIDE
Bowery
Grand St
Grand St
Orchard St
Essex St
E Broadway
Grab a bite with the 'in' crowd at **Dimes** cafe (p72) after skipping down uber-cool Orchard St.
1min walk from East Broadway station
WH Seward Park
Canal St
East Broadway

09 Join the COUNTERCULTURE

MOSAICS | GARDENS | PUNK ROCK

Nonconformist boundary breakers have a long history of sidestepping the mainstream on East Village streets. Activists, anarchists, poets and punks spent years fighting tooth and nail alongside renegade street artists and brazen squatters to keep this neighborhood a rabble-rouser's kingdom. Although changing demographics have softened its bite, there's still plenty of rebellious flavor to savor. Cruise corners where bohemian counterculture rages on.

STEVE TULLEY/ALAMY STOCK PHOTO ©

How to

Getting around Take the 6 to Astor Pl and head east on 8th St. Find community gardens blooming on side streets off Ave C (also called 'Loisaida Ave').

When to go Visit between 1 April and 31 October to explore gardens during public opening hours.

Grab-and-go While strolling the neighborhood, stop by **C&B** (located on the south side of Tompkins Square Park) for a killer egg sandwich. Take it to go; eat on a park bench.

JON BILOUS/SHUTTERSTOCK ©

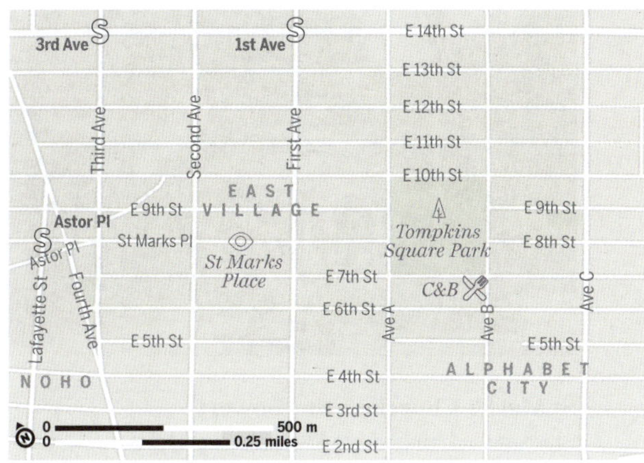

East Village Essences

Find mosaics Wander **St Marks Place** – a three-block strip of 8th St between Astor Pl and Tompkins Square Park – to admire mosaics glued to lampposts, stoops and sidewalks. This is the work of guerrilla artist Jim Power ('the Mosaic Man') – a Vietnam vet who decided to beautify his neighborhood one tile at a time starting in the 1980s. Power believes he created nearly 80 pieces, but NYC officials initially called it vandalism and took many down. They eventually back-pedaled and his mosaics still shine.

Hang in the living room In the 1980s, **Tompkins Square Park** wasn't the pretty pedestrian space it is today – it was an encampment of squatters, who clashed with police in '88 and '91. The squatters are gone, but an anarchist ethos lingers, especially during the annual **Tompkins Square Riot Reunion** concert – an August punk party commemorating the events.

Smell the roses Between spring and autumn, look for flowers blooming behind fences. In the 1970s, abandoned buildings made the Lower East Side an urban war zone – until the Green Guerillas started 'seed bombing' empty lots. Community gardens sprouted in the coming decades, taking root around the neighborhood's low-income, predominantly Latinx section (nicknamed 'Loisaida'). While some gardens have been bulldozed and replaced by new developments, many hold their ground. Find a garden map on the **Loisada United Neighborhood Gardens** website (lungsnyc.org/gardens-greenspaces).

Top left St Marks Place **Bottom left** East Village community garden park

Punks of the Park

Tompkins Square Park's legacy of defiance goes back to the 19th century. In 1857 police sparred with immigrants protesting a lack of food and jobs. The bloody Civil War Draft Riots of 1863 also spilled into the park, and in 1877, 5000 locals faced the billy clubs of National Guardsmen at a Communist rally with revolutionary edge. The park traded gore for glitter at Wigstock – a transgressive drag festival, started in 1984 by drag queen Lady Bunny and immortalized in the 1995 documentary *Wigstock: The Movie*. Things got violent again in 1988, when an imposed curfew (still in place) pissed off the park's punk squatters.

400 Years of East Village Evolution

MAPPING THE NEIGHBORHOOD'S METAMORPHOSIS

East Village old-timers started declaring their bohemian neighborhood 'dead' in the 1980s, a victim of rising rents that threatened to trash the cultural foundation built by immigrants, expats and artists. But over four centuries, change has been an East Village inevitability. Visit destinations central to the neighborhood's narrative, where preservation and transformation intertwine.

Left St Mark's Church in-the-Bowery **Centre** Deutsch-Amerikanische Schützen Gesellschaft **Right** John Varvatos store

St Mark's Church in-the-Bowery

Stare at this church from 1799, which protests the rigidity of 10th St and Second Ave by standing on a diagonal, and imagine NYC before Manhattan's grid (established in 1811) split streets into right angles. In 1651, Petrus Stuyvesant, New Amsterdam's longest-running governor, turned this area into his family's *bouwerij* (Dutch for 'farm'). He added a chapel in 1660, making this NYC's oldest religious site still in use. As New York's street plan took shape, Stuyvesant St (running by the church) was the neighborhood's only dissenting road spared.

German-American Shooting Society

Look above this building's 2nd-floor windows (now a yoga studio) to see a German inscription etched in stone: **Deutsch-Amerikanische Schützen Gesellschaft** *(German-American Shooting Society; 12 St Marks Pl)*, carved in the late 1880s when this area was called Kleindeutschland (Little Germany).

At its peak, roughly 150,000 working-class Germans lived around these blocks – until a mass exodus at the turn of the century shifted demographics. In 1904, NYC faced its deadliest disaster until September 11: the steamship *General Slocum*, caught fire in the East River and sank. An estimated 1021 people died – mainly women and children from Kleindeutschland. Depression plagued the community's survivors, causing many to move elsewhere in the coming years. Architectural relics are all that remains of the neighborhood's German heyday.

Electric Circus

The Lower East Side extended north to 14th St until the 1950s, when artists came east from Greenwich Village

KENNETH GRANT / ALAMY STOCK PHOTO ©

EVERETT COLLECTION INC/ALAMY STOCK PHOTO ©

to settle among cheap apartment buildings populated by Ukrainian and Polish immigrants. Real estate agents followed, rebranding the area between 14th and Houston Sts to mirror its atmospheric western neighbor. In 1964, the *New York Times* printed its new name: the East Village.

The creative revolution was in full swing by 1966, just as art king Andy Warhol transformed the Polish National Home into the **Electric Circus** *(19-25 St Marks Pl)* – a transcendental nightclub. But Warhol's haunt lost its luster in 1970, when a bomb detonated on the dance floor. It closed within a year, just as the area descended into a drugged-up, dilapidated shell of its former self. The site is now a string of restaurants. As for the 'East Village' moniker? It stuck.

CBGB

Step inside leather-scented menswear store **John Varvatos** *(315 Bowery)* and notice the walls. Graffiti and show posters recall when this was CBGB – a bar central to the East Village's rise to music hotspot. From 1973 to 2006, the dingy venue incubated punk and new wave bands like the Ramones and Blondie. It also catapulted the neighborhood into an age of prosperity, enticing developers to capitalize on CBGB's fortunes by transforming surrounding real estate from hardcore grit into high-class gloss.

> The dingy venue incubated punk and new wave bands like the Ramones and Blondie.

The neighborhood's evolution became CBGB's demise. When the bar's landlord demanded a 50% rent increase, it was forced to shut its doors.

Four Decades in Four Songs

Nutty – Live at the Five Spot *(Thelonious Monk Quartet; 1958)* Jazz pianist Monk plays for a buzzing crowd at a cafe central to the neighborhood's artsy transformation.

I'm Waiting For the Man *(Velvet Underground; 1969)* The Electric Circus' house band sings about scoring heroin – just as it exploded on downtown's drug scene.

Life During Wartime *(Talking Heads; 1979)* Lyricist David Byrne's post-apocalyptic poetry, written from a loft on Ave A, captures the anarchy of Alphabet City.

Rent *(Jonathan Larson; 1996)* East Village residents lament how they'll pay rent in the title song from a Broadway musical that mirrors the lives of 1990s squatters.

10 Kvell Over Jewish HISTORY

DELIS | TENEMENTS | MUSEUMS

Between 1881 and 1924, over two million Jews fled Eastern Europe for the US in response to anti-Jewish sentiment. Most settled among NYC'S Lower East Side, and today, the city is home to the largest Jewish population in the country. Spend half a day spotting their imprints around the neighborhood, now permanently sewn into the city's social fabric.

How to

Getting around Take the F/M or J/Z to Delancey St and prepare to walk at least half a mile.

Sidewalk stories Look for faded stars in the pavement on E 10th St and Second Ave's southeast corner (now a Chase Bank) to spot names of Jewish thespians who thrived here pre-WWII. Back then, Second Ave was known as 'Yiddish Broadway.'

Come Hungry Taste Jewish culinary traditions at delis and food counters like Katz's Delicatessen and B&H Dairy while exploring the neighborhood.

Learn, Eat, Pray

Tenement life Briefly inhabit the neighborhood's heart-breaking, hardscrabble and inspiring heritage at the **Tenement Museum** (10am-6pm), which leads small group tours through historically restored tenement apartments. Each tour highlights personal stories of immigrants from who lived here at various points. For a Jewish-centric snapshot, reserve tickets for 'Tenement Women: 1902'. Book tickets in advance.

Eastern Europe's eats Walk five minutes from the Tenement Museum to East Houston St and dine on Jewish deli food – staples of NYC's culinary scene. **Katz's**

Top right Tenement Museum
Bottom right Yonah Schimmel's Knish Bakery

BRIAN LOGAN PHOTOGRAPHY/SHUTTERSTOCK ©

Jewish Bakery & Deli Decoder

Bagel A roll with a hole: boiled in barley malt-mixed water then baked. Order it at **Russ & Daughters**.

Bialy The bagel's Polish cousin – round bread with an indented top, filled with onions or poppy seeds. Try it at **Kossar's Bagels & Bialys**.

Matzo ball soup Eggy dumplings made with matzo (unleavened bread) and dunked in steamy chicken broth. Slurp it down at **B&H Dairy**.

Blintz A crepe-style wrap, often stuffed with a sweetened cheese like ricotta, topped with fruit compote or possibly sour cream.

Delicatessen (established 1888) serves one of the best pastrami sandwiches in town. Prices are steep but sandwiches are huge. Three blocks west is **Yonah Schimmel's Knish Bakery**, which started selling its namesake Jewish dough pockets from a Coney Island pushcart in the 1890s. By 1910, the store opened here.

Religious sanctuary End with a visit to the **Museum at Eldridge Street** (10am-5pm Sun-Fri), a Moorish-Gothic-Romanesque synagogue from 1887 that once served as a center for Lower East Side Jewish life. After circling the small basement museum, head upstairs to admire the stained-glass centerpiece.

DW LABS INCORPORATED/SHUTTERSTOCK ©

11 Cruise Stylish ORCHARD ST

STROLLING | EATING | SHOPPING

Designer duds, fine art, quirky boutiques and happening restaurants – find it all on Orchard St. There was an actual orchard here in the early 1700s, followed by tenement buildings, vendor-operated pushcarts and textile storefronts in the late 1800s. Nowadays, the stretch between Houston and Canal Sts is the Lower East Side's hippest thoroughfare.

ROBERT K CHIN - STOREFRONTS/ALAMY STOCK PHOTO ©

Trip Notes

Getting here Take the F to Second Ave and walk east to the intersection of E Houston and Orchard Sts. From there, head south toward Canal St.

When to go Explore around midday. Plan to eat lunch at Scarr's Pizza.

Nearby nabes Plenty of neighborhoods are accessible from here: head west toward Chinatown for dumplings, walk the Manhattan Bridge for East River views or grab drinks around Dime Sq.

Debating Dimes Square

Real micro 'hood or passing fad? A few years ago, popular media named this triangle around Division and Canal Sts the place to go for lunching among models and imbibing among skaters. What we know for sure: **Dimes** restaurant is its epicenter – and it's delicious, if you can get a table.

FROM LEFT: FORGET PATRICK / ALAMY STOCK PHOTO ©, BJANKA KADIC / ALAMY STOCK PHOTO ©

12 Innovative ARTISTS

MUSIC | THEATER | COCKTAILS

When darkness descends, these neighborhoods shine bright with talent-packed stages and mixologist-led bars. The creative legacy here goes back decades: this is where the Talking Heads made waves in the sonic landscape, where a young RuPaul Charles commanded crowds, where *Rent* paid its dues and where a cocktail craze bubbled up in the early aughts. Spend a night quaffing the latest cultural trends.

How to

Getting here You'll find performance venues sprinkled around both the East Village and the Lower East Side. East Houston is the dividing line: take the F to Second Ave to be at its epicenter.

When to go These are all post-dinner activities. Shows generally start at 7pm; some will kick off at midnight. Cocktail bars close between 1am and 4am.

Reserve a spot Purchase tickets and reserve bar seats in advance or you might find yourself out of luck.

Stage Time

Inventive variety Broadway might have splashy shows, but downtown is where you'll spot some of the city's most original, risk-ready theatrical minds. If you're into circus performers, burlesque artists or ribald comedians, see who's on stage at the **Slipper Room** (slipperroom.com), an intimate 2nd-floor theater. If you want to see Broadway's next big thing before the crowds catch on, check out **New York Theatre Workshop** (NYTW; nwtw.org), an incubator for musicals like *Rent* and *Hadestown* before they went mainstream.

Rock on the rise Rock and pop up-and-comers have

Top right Slipper Room
Bottom right Mercury Lounge

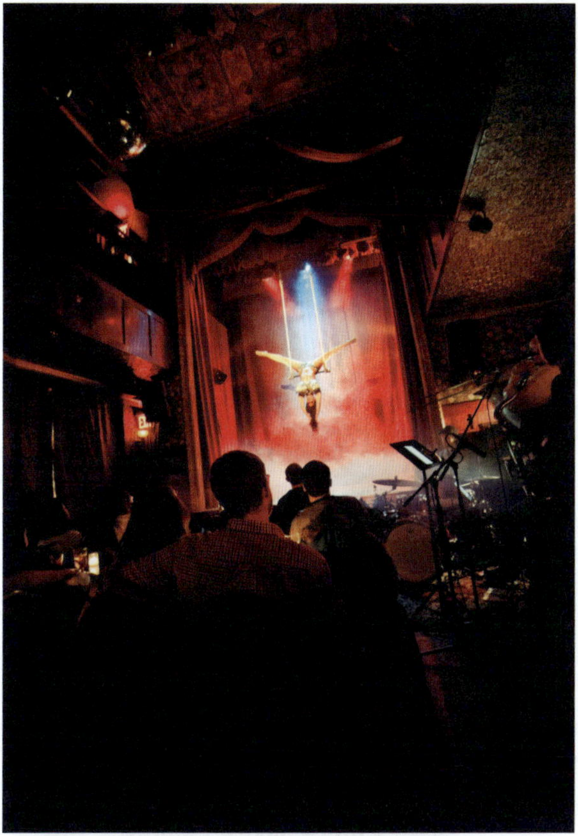

CITIZENBURLESQUE./WIKIMEDIA/C BY-SA 4.0 ©

ROBERT K. CHIN - STOREFRONTS / ALAMY STOCK PHOTO ©

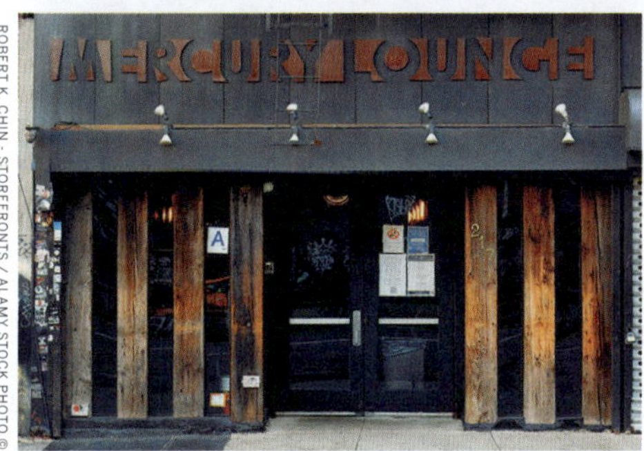

Classy Cocktails

NYC's mixology revolution technically began at Midtown's **Rainbow Room**, where bartender Dale DeGroff became 'daddy' of the 1990s craft cocktail craze, but it earned international recognition after taking off here in the early 2000s. Bartenders have been mixing bespoke beverages at **Death & Co** since 2006, and couples have been entering speakeasy **PDT** through a Crif Dogs telephone booth since 2007. There's a dizzying amount of new juice joints, too: **Double Chicken Please** was named 2023's Best Bar in the US by the World's 50 Best organization.

wailed behind the art deco facade at the **Bowery Ballroom** since 1998, along with big names like Patti Smith and Lady Gaga. Sister venue **Mercury Lounge** (mercuryeastpresents.com) sticks to indie artists.

Informal favorites Getting tickets to some of these shows can be tough. You'll still find plenty of shows at non-ticketed or casual venues – and though the budgets will be significantly smaller for these slapdash spectacles, you might spot the next household name. Try LGBTIQ+ bar **Club Cumming** for cabaret, comedy and drag. **Bowery Poetry Club** is the place to go for spoken word.

Listings

BEST OF THE REST

Imported Flavors & Food Stalls

Veselka $$

This beloved vestige of the area's Ukrainian past has been serving handmade *varenyky* (cheese, potato or meat dumplings; also called pierogis), borscht and goulash since 1954.

Essex Market $$

Browse stalls selling cheese, groceries, spices, Dominican food, ceviche, rice balls and more. Home to **Shopsin's** (inventive diner fare) and **Dhamaka** (spicy Indian).

Yellow Rose $$

Flour tortillas give Tex-Mex taquerias their north-of-the-border flair, which is what you'll get at this far-north-of-Texas outpost. Try the bean-and-cheese taco.

Plant-based Bites

Superiority Burger $$

The best veggie burger in town, certainly, but don't sleep on this punk-rock diner's other delicious bangers, including mouthwatering pies and flavor-packed sides (get the sweet potato).

Punjabi Grocery & Deli $

If you spot yellow taxis parked out front, you're in the right place. Former cabbie Kulwinder Singh opened this no-frills food counter in 1993, serving home-cooked Punjabi-style plates.

Dirt Candy $$$

Snag a reservation at this classy, grassy Michelin-starred restaurant and the vegetable-forward tasting menu will make you forget you ever liked meat.

Sweet Treats & Breakfast

Smør Bakery $

Watch as bakers knot dough to create cardamom buns, served warm from the oven at this Scandinavian-style baker, which also serves stand-out sandwiches, toasts and savory rolls.

Librae Bakery $

The combination of Middle Eastern ingredients and Danish baking techniques results in fabulous concoctions like za'atar labneh morning buns and pistachio rose croissants.

Iced Coffee & Espresso

Abraço $

Find a table inside this ground-level cafe to sip perfectly prepared espresso drinks while inhaling the dangerously addictive olive-oil cake.

Lê Phin $

Enjoy a taste of Hanoi by ordering the Vietnamese iced coffee made with condensed milk or the pandan matcha latte with house-made pandan syrup.

Bitters, Sake & Liquors

Amor y Amargo $$

'Love and Bitters' is a cocktail chemistry lab showcasing its namesake amaro selection. Walk through the vintage apothecary entrance to the tasting room, where bartenders offer advice on flavors.

Accidental Bar $$

The sake sommeliers behind this Japanese juice joint inspire indulgence. Sip styles with descriptions like 'drinking gin with a delightful Swamp Witch.'

Attaboy $$$

Speakeasy vibes and bespoke cocktails – just tell the barkeep what you like, and they'll whip up the concoction of your dreams. Pricey but exceptional.

Wine & Beer Bars

Parkside Lounge $

Old-school dive bar where bros chug beers while hitting billiard balls. Gay disco party **Wet Noise** occasionally crowds the dark back room with sweaty dancers.

Proletariat $$

Craft brew cognoscenti sidle up to this slender bar for 'rare, new and unusual beer' served alongside plant-based small plates.

Parcelle $$$

Wine comes first at this oenophile outlet, followed closely by design. Peep at the embroidered mushroom mural, corduroy chairs and snaking leather sofa.

Ruffian $$$

If you're into orange wines and mostly vegetarian fare, grab a stool at this intimate wine joint to taste Eastern European grapes while watching the chef work bar-side magic.

Fashionable Threads

Only NY

Forget the 'I Love NY' shirts – this street-smart, normcore independent fashion store's line of city merch celebrates city sites and organizations, each piece dripping with local swagger.

Country Of

The '80s and '90s are alive inside this snug vintage shop known for its curated collection of American, European and Japanese designer pieces ranging from Levi's to Gaultier.

Paperbacks & Posters

Bluestockings Cooperative Bookstore

Come to this collectively-run community space – named after Enlightenment feminists – for books by queer, trans and sex-worker authors.

Mast Books

Peruse piles of rare and out-of-print titles at this bookstore and art gallery. Check their Instagram for upcoming author talks, book launches and signings.

Fine Art, Film & History

New Museum

The original building, a series of off-kilter building blocks, went up in 2007. A futuristic OMA-designed extension is slated for early 2025 – fitting for the contemporary works on display.

Metrograph

Indie movie house equipped with state-of-the-art digital projectors, an old 35mm reel-to-reel and an upstairs restaurant. Check for premieres, classic oldies and rare archival films.

Museum of Reclaimed Urban Space

Visit this former tenement building reclaimed by squatters in the 1980s to learn about grassroots urban activists fighting against corporate power in the East Village and beyond.

Steam & Sauna

Russian & Turkish Baths

Schvitz (sweat) with an eclectic mix of actors, students, couples, singles, Orthodox Jews and blissed-out granddads. Most hours are coed (clothing required); some are men- and women-only (clothing optional).

WEST VILLAGE & CHELSEA

ARTSY | CHARMING | HISTORIC

WEST VILLAGE & CHELSEA
Trip Builder

TAKE YOUR PICK OF MUST-SEES AND HIDDEN GEMS

The West Village is a maze of tree-lined streets brimming with brownstones and intimate restaurants. Further west is the Hudson River, hugged by a gorgeous green park. North is Chelsea, with galleries galore. Originally a hub for immigrants, artists and LGBTIQ+ crowds, well-healed Manhattanites now covets these picturesque neighborhoods.

Neighborhood Notes

Best for Art, dining, drinking and parks.

Transportation A/C/E or 1/2/3 to 14th St – the Village and Chelsea's border.

Getting around The West Village is west of Sixth Ave; Greenwich Village is east of Sixth Ave.

Tip Use GPS to navigate winding West Village streets – even locals get lost.

0 500 m
0 0.25 miles

W 26th St
W 25th St
23rd St
W 22nd St
W 21st St

Skip between starchitect-designed high-rises and blooming gardens on the elevated esplanade of the **High Line** (p84).

9min walk from 14th St/Eighth Ave station

Listen to brass bands blow their horns at the **Village Vanguard** (p92), a jazz hall from the 1930s.

2min walk from 14th St/ Seventh Ave station

Descend into the **Comedy Cellar** (p92), where stand-ups test new material on tables of tittering guests.

2min from W 4th St station

Dine, drink and shop for artisanal wares inside steampunk-style **Chelsea Market** (p86), a former Nabisco factory.

4min walk from 14th St/ Eighth Ave station

Reserve a table at award-winning Indian restaurant **Semma** (p96) to see how much spice you can handle.

3min walk from 14th St/Seventh Ave station

People-watch at lively **Washington Square Park** (p95), a popular green space atop an 18th-century graveyard.

2min walk from W 4th St station

Clink glasses inside the **Stonewall Inn** (p91), where a 1969 uprising changed the course of LGBTIQ+ history.

1min walk from Christopher St station

Belt Broadway tunes with musical theater aficionados at piano bar **Marie's Crisis** (p97).

6min walk from Christopher St station

Ninth Ave
UNION SQUARE
Gansevoort St
Greenwich Ave
Greenwich St
Hudson St
Eighth Ave
Bank St
Sixth Ave (Avenue of the Americas)
Seventh Ave
W 4th St
W 10th St
Christopher St
W 8th St
Waverly Pl
Washington Sq N
Christopher St-Sheridan Sq
Sheridan Sq
Grove St
Washington Pl
Washington Square Park
Washington Sq E
W 4th St
Washington Sq S
W 4th St-Washington Sq
Bleecker St
WEST VILLAGE
GREENWICH VILLAGE

13 PIER HOP in Hudson River Park

WATERFRONT | RECREATION | OUTDOORS

Hudson River Park is the 550-acre shining star of Manhattan's modern green spaces, transforming a former industrial wasteland into a pedestrian playground – a 4-mile ribbon running along the waterfront from Tribeca to Hell's Kitchen. Spend an afternoon pier hopping along its prettiest section, linking the Village and Chelsea.

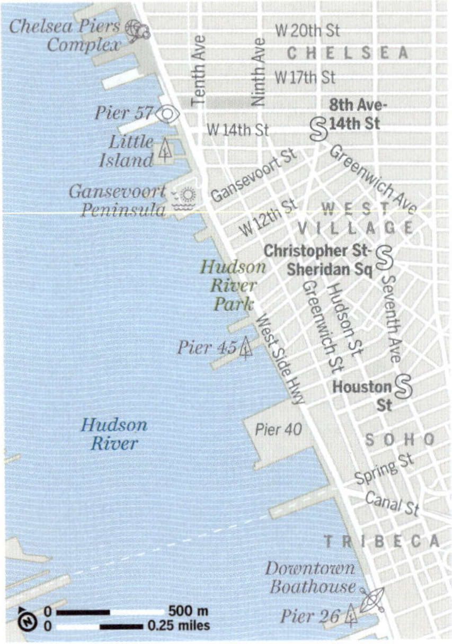

How to

Getting here Take the 1 to Christopher St for Pier 45. Take the A/C/E or L to 14 St for Little Island. Walk west to the water.

When to go Save this for sunny days between spring and autumn. Sunsets are spectacular.

Cycle the strip A 13-mile bike path passes through this park before continuing along Manhattan's west side. Rent wheels to conquer the entire trail (bikerent.nyc) or use bike share program Citi Bike to pedal smaller sections.

Pick Your Pier

Pier 45 Known colloquially as Christopher St Pier, this 900ft wharf connects the waterfront to what used to be the heart of LGBTIQ+ life in the West Village. In the 1970s and early '80s, gay men gathered on dilapidated docks for sunbathing and sexual experimentation. The scene is much more family-friendly today, though you'll still find speedo-clad visitors soaking in vitamin D.

Gansevoort Peninsula Grab a chair on this sandy slip, completed in 2023 and billed as 'Manhattan's first public beach,' and admire David Hammons' ghostly *Day's End*. The 52ft-high, 325ft-long art installation – a skeletal warehouse – evokes the park's industrial past.

Top right Pier 57 **Bottom right** Gansevoort Peninsula

GRAPHIKLINE/SHUTTERSTOCK ©

RBLFMR/SHUTTERSTOCK ©

Cruise or Kayak

See NYC from a sailor's perspective by hopping on a boat at sports-and-entertainment complex **Chelsea Piers**. The American Institute of Architects (AIA) and Classic Harbor Line team up for a fun, informative cruise (around three hours) aboard a 1920s-style commuter yacht that circumnavigates Manhattan. Tickets include a complimentary drink ($116/86 adult/student; sail-nyc.com). If you prefer a free floating experience, paddle around Tribeca's **Pier 26** on a kayak provided by **Downtown Boathouse** (downtownboathouse.org), offered Saturdays and Sundays from mid-May to mid-October.

Little Island (littleisland.org) This architectural triumph appeared as a surrealist dream in 2021: 132 concrete pods shoot from the water, crowned by undulating green hills. Stroll the 2.4-acre folly's footpaths to enjoy gentle breezes and expansive views. Check the seasonal event schedule for live performances; tickets to the amphitheater are all capped at $25.

Pier 57 Round out the day with a range of entertainment options at Pier 57: live music at **City Winery**, food vendors at **Market 57** and a rooftop great for sunset views.

14 Amble Along the HIGH LINE

ARCHITECTURE | GREEN SPACE

Snaking between Hudson Yards and the Meatpacking District at 30ft above street level, the High Line is a fabulous example of industrial reuse. Once a freight line linking slaughterhouses, it's now a green ribbon where you can wander along urban gardens and glossy towers to the Whitney – a museum featuring modern American art.

PIT STOCK /SHUTTERSTOCK ©

How to

Getting here/around Take the A/C/E to 34th St Penn Station or the 7 to 34th St Hudson Yards. Start at 34th St in Midtown and head 1.5 miles south to Gansevoort St in the Meatpacking District.

When to go Early morning is best – crowds cause congestion on sunny weekend afternoons.

Top tip Download the Bloomberg Connects app for in-depth info on the High Line's art and gardens.

Rails to Real Estate

The High Line's story begins in the early 20th century when perilous street-level tracks served the west side's booming industrial enterprises, earning Tenth Ave the nickname 'Death Avenue.' A two-story-high railway became the expensive solution, and the 'West Side Elevated Line' ran its first train in 1933. It wasn't long before the train line became a money pit and fell into disuse; in the 1990s, demolition was mooted.

Enter the Friends of the High Line, whose vision of an elegant, elevated park slowly caught on. Years of activism resulted in the jewel enjoyed today: a pedestrian catwalk planted with 500-plus native species that wends its way above the area's former factories and through canyons of top-dollar luxury towers.

PIT STOCK/SHUTTERSTOCK ©

Top The High Line **Bottom** The High Line

Saunter South on the High Line

Begin your journey near Hudson Yards (enter at 30th or 34th Sts), with supertall skyscrapers shining eastward and the Hudson River rolling to the west. Plant-packed railroad tracks evoke the industrial wilderness that preceded the park's creation.

As the path narrows, you'll see tons of towers by world-famous starchitects. There's Zaha Hadid's futuristic glass-and-metal apartment complex at **520 West 28th Street**, Thomas Heatherwick's bulbous bay-windowed **Lantern House** (he also designed the controversial *Vessel* at Hudson Yards) and Bjarke Ingels' **One High Line** (a pair of twisted buildings frozen in a tango).

For a bird's-eye view of Tenth Ave, sit on amphitheater-style seats at 17th or 26th Sts and watch cabs zoom by below. If you prefer serene scenery, snag one of the river-facing chaise lounges on the **Diller-von Furstenberg Sundeck** – named after fashion queen Diane

Chelsea Market's Artisanal Treats

Exit the High Line at 15th St and you'll be outside **Chelsea Market** – a bustling urban bazaar occupying a former Nabisco factory. Over three dozen vendors ply their temptations throughout, including **Los Mariscos** (to-die-for ceviche), the **Lobster Place** (good luck resisting their rolls), **Fat Witch Bakery** (brownies and other decadent hits) and **Day Drinks** (on-tap espressos, teas and botanicals). If you want outdoor seating, head to the covered sidewalk tables. Once you've had your fill, check out **Artists & Fleas** – a small market where local artists sell their wares. There's a spacious public restroom in the basement.

Eat Spanish at Hudson Yards

Hudson Yards' shiny skyscrapers are the architectural exclamation point to the High Line's northern end – largely reviled by critics upon opening in 2019. Regardless of interpretation, you'll likely be charmed by **Mercado Little Spain**, a series of high-end Iberian-style food stalls on the lower level of a shopping mall.

18TH STUDIO/SHUTTERSTOCK ©

VIEW PICTURES/GETTY IMAGES ©

von Furstenberg and her billionaire husband Barry Diller, the pockets behind this entire project.

Food vendors at 22nd St and 15th St open from May to October, serving grab-and-go goodies like Belgian fries, donuts and tamales.

Explore the Whitney

The **Whitney Museum of American Art** anchors the southern end of the High Line with a glass-and-cement structure designed by architect Renzo Piano. It looks like a gleaming factory and giant cruise ship mash-up – fitting for its location along the Hudson River's former industrial, ship-lined shores. Outdoor terraces lead to a smattering of sculptures and skyline views.

Rotating exhibits are generally exceptional, showcasing some of the biggest artists du jour, but if you're short on time, beeline to the 7th floor's permanent collection. The selection of works by American all-stars is astounding: there's Edward Hopper, Jasper Johns, Georgia O'Keeffe, Andy Warhol and more artists who spent time creating in NYC. Admission is free on Friday (5pm-10pm) and the second Sunday of every month.

LEONARD ZHUKOVSKY/SHUTTERSTOCK ©

Left 520 West 28th Street
Top right Chelsea Market
Bottom right Mercado Little Spain

15 ADMIRE ART at Chelsea's Galleries

CONTEMPORARY ART | CULTURE | WALKING TOUR

Zigzagging through far-west Chelsea in the afternoon is like visiting a sprawling art museum. The area is home to NYC's densest concentration of galleries, and unlike the Whitney or MoMA, visiting these showrooms is gratis. Join the city's well-heeled aesthetes by hunting the streets for a visual feast.

A ASTES/ALAMY STOCK PHOTO ©

Trip Notes

Getting around Take the A/C/E to 34th St-Penn Station or the 7 to 34th St-Hudson Yards to start at High Line Nine. Walking between galleries covers a little under a mile.

When to go Hours vary, but most galleries open from 10am to 6pm Tuesday to Saturday.

Food break Refuel inside **Tía Pol**, a tapas spot serving Basque-inspired small plates. A weekday happy hour from 3pm to 6pm tailors to the gallery-going crowd.

Gasoline to Galleries

Far-west Chelsea was better known as Gasoline Alley in the early 1990s, when mechanics genuflected before hulking vehicles. That slowly changed once the art crowd moved in. Eduardo Kobra's vibrant *Mount Rushmore* mural on 22nd St and 10th Ave showcases the gods of today's ruling class: Warhol, Kahlo, Haring, Basquiat.

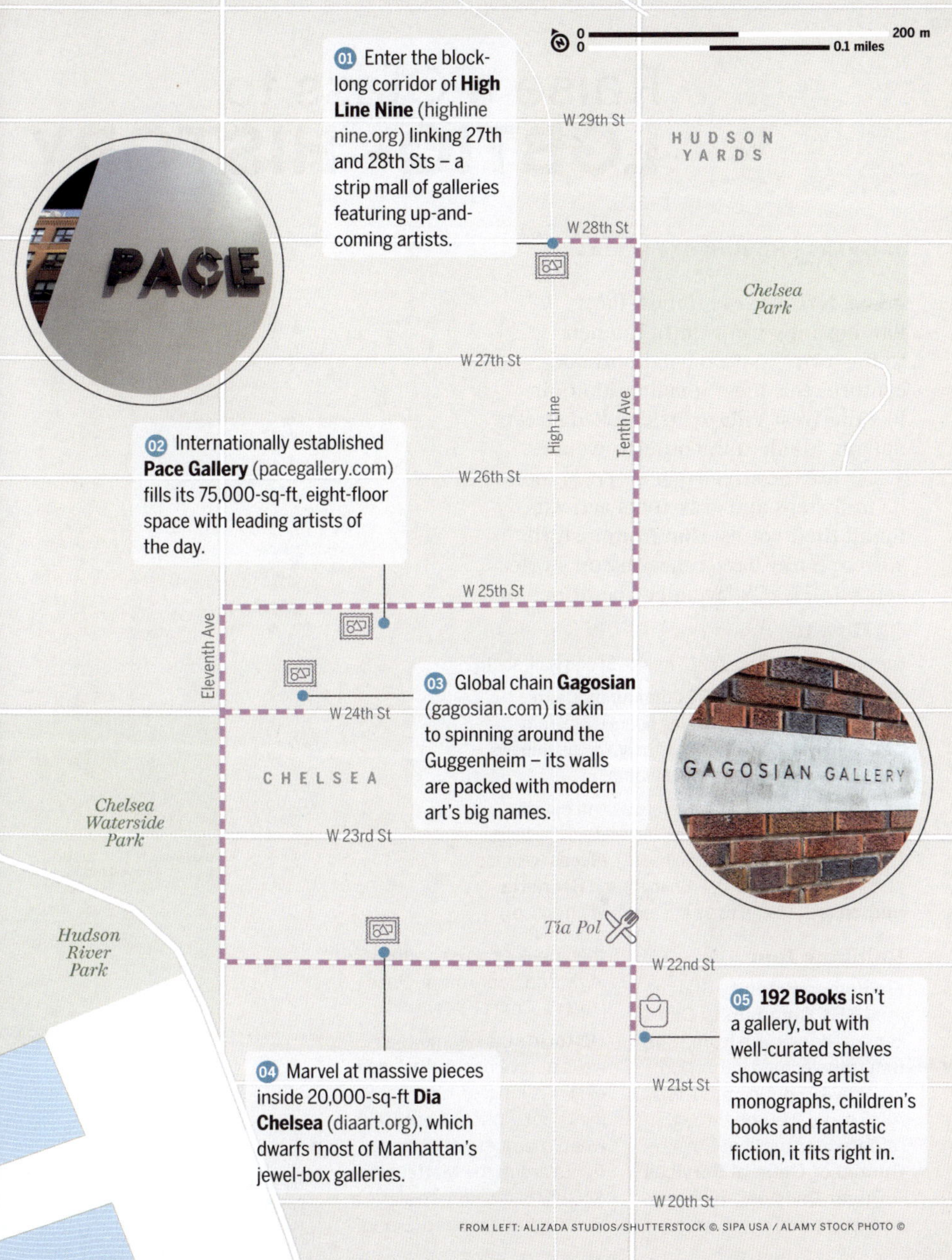

FROM LEFT: ALIZADA STUDIOS/SHUTTERSTOCK ©, SIPA USA / ALAMY STOCK PHOTO ©

16 Raise a Glass to LGBTIQ+ HISTORY

GAY BARS | MONUMENTS | PRIDE

NYC waves rainbow flags flamboyantly from Hell's Kitchen to Bushwick, but no neighborhood captures the queer imagination quite like the West Village, its crooked streets defying Manhattan's orderly avenues. These are the streets where Pride took its first steps and grassroots activists found their voices. Hop from historic sites to buzzy bars, reflecting on stories central to NYC's lavender liberation.

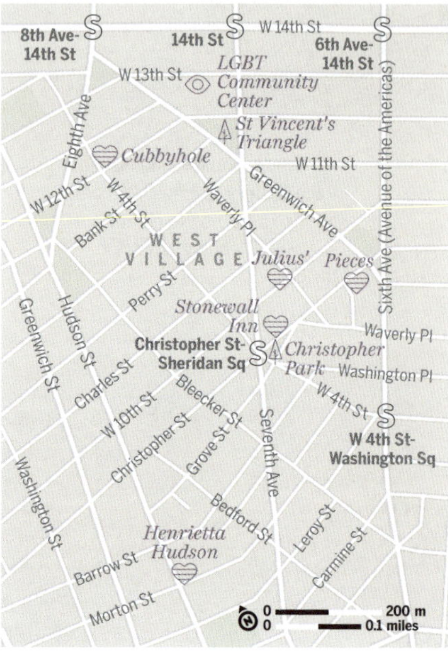

How to

Getting here Take the 1/2/3 to 14th St and walk south.

When to go Visit the **LGBT Community Center** during its bookstore's opening hours (1pm-7pm Wed-Sun). June is particularly lively, when rainbows decorate storefronts for Pride month.

Bar hop Turn this experience into a night out by skipping between the Village's many LGBTIQ+ bars. Try **Cubbyhole** (cozy lesbian haunt), **Pieces** (visit for performances by Kiki Ball-Change) and **Henrietta Hudson** (self-identifies as a 'queer human space'.)

Rainbow Tour

Finding community Start at the **LGBT Community Center**, a schoolhouse from 1848 that transformed into a hub for activism during the 1980s AIDS crisis. Thumb through rainbow-centric lit at the **Bureau of General Services – Queer Division**, an on-site bookstore and event space, then peek at artist Keith Haring's 2nd floor mural, *Once Upon a Time* (1989).

Historic sips Search the walls at dive bar **Julius'**, one of NYC's longest-running gay joints, for a photo from 1966 when members of early gay rights group the Mattachine Society came here to stage a Civil Rights–inspired 'Sip-In,'

Top right Stonewall Inn
Bottom right Queer Liberation March

LITTLE VIGNETTES PHOTO/SHUTTERSTOCK ©

RON ADAR/SHUTTERSTOCK ©

 Pride in June

When NYC's inaugural Pride march erupted in 1970 to commemorate the Stonewall rebellion, it was a day-long protest spanning 50 blocks. It's now a month-long party in all five boroughs, ending on June's last Sunday with one of the world's biggest LGBTIQ+ parades. The week before the parade is jam-packed with events – both family-friendly and downright debaucherous. To lean into Pride's rebellious origins, consider attending the **Queer Liberation March**. For official Pride events, visit nycpride.org.

protesting a discriminatory law against serving alcohol to gays and lesbians.

LGBTIQ+ rights movement
Stroll two minutes from Julius' to reach the symbolic heart of NYC's queer community – the **Stonewall Inn**, where an infamous police raid on 28 June 1969 sparked an uprising that changed the course of the LGBTIQ+ rights movement. Raise a glass to activists like Marsha P Johnson at today's incarnation of the original bar, visit the welcome center (informative but sterile, added in 2024), then meditate on the movement's half-century of progress inside adjacent **Christopher Park** – central to the **Stonewall National Monument**, designated in 2016.

Downtown's LIVE ARTS SCENE

JAZZ | COMEDY | THEATER

Greenwich Village started buzzing with bohemian revelry in the early 20th century, when starving artists colonized its cheap tenements for their creative pursuits. It soon became synonymous with the avant garde, and over the next century, performance venues sprang up showcasing the neighborhood's boundary-breaking intelligentsia. Kick back in a jazz joint, comedy club or experimental theater that carries on the tradition.

How to

Getting around Take the 1/2/3 to 14th St for the Village Vanguard. Take the A/C/E or B/D/F/M to West 4th St for the Comedy Cellar.

When to go Most performances start in the evening, but if you plan ahead, it's possible to see more than one performance in a day. Try a weekend theater matinee followed by an early evening jazz show and, if you've got the energy, a late-night comedy set.

Superior Stages

Brass Bands New Orleans might be the birthplace of jazz, but by the 1930s, NYC became the art form's heartland. Impressive riffs still echo at the prestigious **Village Vanguard** (villagevanguard.com), which has hosted every major star since opening in 1935. Turn a quiet Monday night into a big-band jamboree by seeing the Vanguard Jazz Orchestra. Downbeats begin at 8pm and 10pm.

Laughing Fits In the 1950s and '60s, a form of confrontational stand-up comedy emerged in Village cafes. You'll find the movement's funny-bone-baring descendants at the **Comedy Cellar**

Top right Cafe Wha?
Bottom right Cherry Lane Theatre

Slapstick to Stand-up

NYC's modern comedy scene began on 19th-century vaudeville stages, with slapstick performances playing to back rows of big theaters. These bits continued into the 1940s, as emcees cracked middlebrow jokes to supper-club crowds. Things morphed in the 1950s, when performers took to cozy stages in Village coffee shops like **Cafe Wha?** (still open), where audiences craved conversational, confessional routines. This is how the contemporary stand-up comedian was born – with names like Lenny Bruce, Woody Allen and Joan Rivers forging a style popular today.

(comedycellar.com). Talented regulars started testing new material inside this chuckle den in the 1980s. There are usually several hour-long shows per day.

Proscenium Performers

Theater around the Village distinguishes itself from Broadway by producing out-of-the-box works in intimate spaces. The **Cherry Lane** opened in 1923 and has since shepherded works by playwrights including Lorraine Hansbury, Edward Albee and Sam Shepard. It's also worth seeing what's playing at the **Lucille Lortel** (lortel.org), showcasing works by stars on the rise since 1955.

18 Greet Ghosts of THE VILLAGE

LEGENDS | HAUNTINGS | HISTORY

There are a few things nearly every New Yorker fears: the smell of an empty subway car, an at-home encounter with the city's rat population and getting caught up in Santacon – NYC's most hated holiday tradition. As for the ghosts – they're not so scary, once you get to know them. Tour the Village and Chelsea to meet their permanent residents.

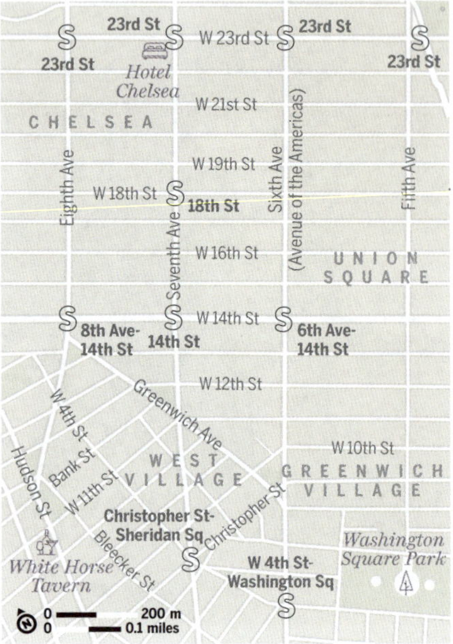

How to

Getting around Take the 1 or C/E to 23rd St for the Hotel Chelsea. Walking between destinations covers 1.5 miles.

When to go October is best: it's spooky season in the Village, when the neighborhood dons some serious Halloween drag.

Who you gonna call? 1984 film *Ghostbusters,* about NYC's paranormal patrol, was partially shot in Manhattan. If you don't have the fictional parapsychologists on speed dial, head to their on-screen HQ at Tribeca's **Hook & Ladder 8** fire station.

Paranormal New York

Haunted house The Queen Anne-Gothic-style **Hotel Chelsea**, completed in 1884, became a bohemian commune in the mid-20th century as tenants like Bob Dylan and Patti Smith took up residence. It's now a boutique hotel – and while most guests check in for a few nights, legend says some never leave. The most famous perpetual guest is Nancy Spungen – stabbed to death on the building's 1st floor in 1978. Her boyfriend, Sex Pistols bassist Sid Vicious, was charged with the murder but died of a heroin overdose before trial.

Top right Washington Square Park **Bottom right** White Horse Tavern

ANDRES GARCIA MARTIN/SHUTTERSTOCK ©

ALIZADA STUDIOS /SHUTTERSTOCK ©

Halloween in the Village

Every October, gourds appear on West Village stoops – all in time for the **Village Halloween Parade**, when costumed covens crawl up Sixth Ave after dark on 31 October. The event started as a grassroots street party in the '70s, fueled by local artists and theater folk; it now attracts upwards of 50,000 participants and hoards of spectators. While the event has gone mainstream, its centerpiece remains the giant handmade puppets that dance through the streets.

Death by drink The **White Horse Tavern** – a storied saloon for literary greats since opening in 1880 – became a haunt for Welsh poet Dylan Thomas in the 1950s. Rumor says his demise was heavy drinking. Dine near his portrait, which hangs near the bar – still waiting for a final serving of spirits.

Underground ghosts Nab a bench in **Washington Square Park** and you'll spot NYU students, street vendors, socializing canines, speed-chess pros, brassy buskers – and ghosts, possibly. From the 1790s to 1820s, this buzzy park was a potter's field – a public graveyard for the poor and forgotten. Over 20,000 souls rest beneath the soil.

Listings

BEST OF THE REST

Critically Acclaimed Restaurants

Semma $$$

Experience summer in South India by ordering the spicy chutneys and sauces on Semma's menu (if you can snag a reservation). Lingering heat from each dish will make you sweat.

Minetta Tavern $$$

Initially opened in 1937, this tavern was frequented by literary bohemians like EE Cummings. A cozy 2009 renovation nods to the original. The Black Label Burger is a smoky sensation.

Taco Style

Los Tacos No 1 $

Chelsea Market is the original home of this NYC chain, serving authentic Mexican tacos filled with meat or *nopal* (grilled cactus). Ask for *con todo* to get all the fixings.

Taco Mahal $

Mix Mexican tacos with Indian flavors to get this 'Lat-India' cuisine: handheld treats made with flatbread (roti or naan) stuffed with servings of palak paneer, curried meat and more.

Mediterranean Meals

Shukette $$$

The fluffy pita is an enticing teaser for what's to come: dollops of labneh, tahini and baba ganoush, then crispy eggplant, Arctic char meatballs and more Middle Eastern delicacies.

Anixi $$

Forget those patchouli-scented vegan dens of the '90s. This faux-meat fortress is dressed to impress with velvet curtains and crystal chandeliers, as fancy as its Mediterranean-inspired menu.

Qanoon $$

Palestinian restaurants are rare in NYC, and Qanoon (an alternative spelling for 'grill' in Arabic) is the best place to try the cuisine's dips, vegetables and meats.

Brunch & Baked Goods

Banter $$

This cheery Australian brunch-lunch hang is ideal for coffee, cocktails, colorful veggie bowls and loaded avocado toast. As for its two outposts, a mile apart? That's what Aussies call 'ace.'

Hector's Cafe & Diner $

Time stands still at this humble, reasonably priced diner hunkered below the High Line. Join wise guys, construction crews and the odd tourist with plates of pancakes, omelets and burgers.

Magnolia Bakery $

This popular chain's original Bleecker St location has seen its buttercream-topped cupcakes on TV and film – but the real star is the banana pudding.

Wine, Beer & Booze Bars

St Jardim $$

Perched on a lively Village side street with oversized windows and outdoor tables, this all-day cafe and natural wine bar is perfect for people-watching while sharing small plates.

124 Old Rabbit Club $

Your reward for finding this well-concealed craft-beer haunt (hint: look for the word

'Rabbit' over the door): rare imported brews and local greats, like Brooklyn-based Grimm Artisanal Ales.

Classy Cocktails

Employees Only $$$

This divine speakeasy-style bar ushered in a new era of haute mixology when it served its first egg-white cocktail in 2004, and it still sets the standard.

Little Branch $$

Walking downstairs to this basement den is a Prohibition throwback: patrons clink glasses and sip artfully prepared cocktails while live jazz occasionally accompanies the percussion of hard-working mixologists.

LGBTIQ+ Mainstays

Marie's Crisis $

Join the chorus at this all-are-welcome, cash-only basement piano dive where show tunes never cease. There's no shortage of Broadway queens and eager chorus kids to lead the communal belting brigade.

Eagle NYC $$

Leather fetishists and jock-strapped himbos cruise this three-level sleaze palace while dancing and drinking with abandon. Come for summer's Sunday beer blasts, when bears down brews on the roof.

Coffee, Tea & Cookies

Té Company

If you prefer oolongs to lattes, you've come to the right place. Loose-leaf teas from farmers in Asia get served alongside sweets so pretty they belong in a Wes Anderson film.

Yanni's Coffee

Get lured into this java counter by the nutty nose of drip coffee (made with beans from Brooklyn's SEY Coffee) and the buttery scent of fresh-baked cookies, dangerously delectable.

Vintage Pieces & Global Fashion

Screaming Mimis

If you dig vintage, designer and flamboyant costume threads, you might scream, too. This funtastic shop carries an excellent selection of yesteryear pieces, organized by decade.

Pippin Vintage Jewelry

These bangles, baubles, brooches and beads might look like a million bucks, but they're mainly under $100. Curious about heritage? Check the tag for a year.

Cueva

A streetside sandwich board showcases the eclectic, stand-out designs represented by this seasonally curated menswear collection, circling the globe from the US to Sweden to Japan.

Zuri

Colorful racks of one-style-fits-all dresses make this Bleecker St shop stand out. Derived from the Swahili word for 'good,' Zuri lives up to its name with ethically sourced clothes from Kenya.

Paperbacks, Notepads & Prints

Goods for the Study

Hardcore journalers and sketch-pad savants go ga-ga for the assortment of paper and writing utensils on display at this den for desk goodies.

Printed Matter, Inc

Don't expect anything carried by mainstream bookstores. Instead, trim shelves hide thousands of ideas packed into strange little zines and limited-edition artist monographs.

MIDTOWN

BUSTLING | BRIGHT | NONSTOP

MARRIOTT MARQUIS
BOB MARLEY
ONE LOVE
ONLY IN THEATRES
FEBRUARY 14
ICON
MARRIOTT MARQUIS
MAGENTA

MIDTOWN
Trip Builder

TAKE YOUR PICK OF MUST-SEES AND HIDDEN GEMS

Midtown is massive. At its center shimmers Times Square, long mythologized as the 'Crossroads of the World,' and what non-New Yorkers often picture as NYC's emblem: commerce, crowds and around-the-clock entertainment. Cloud-piercing architecture dominates the landscape, along with international restaurants, Gilded Age relics and the bright lights of Broadway.

Neighborhood Notes

Best for Theater, architecture, museums

Transportation Every subway line runs through Midtown except for the G.

Getting around Midtown spans 59th to 34th Sts between the Hudson and East Rivers. Use subways for long distances, otherwise travel on foot.

Tip Don't like crowds? Avoid Times Square around Seventh and Eighth Aves.

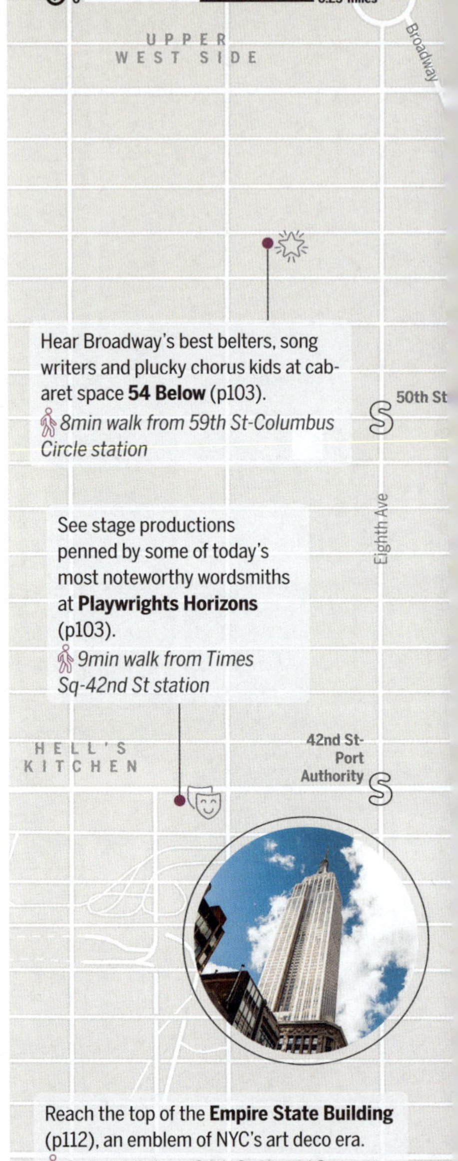

Hear Broadway's best belters, song writers and plucky chorus kids at cabaret space **54 Below** (p103).
8min walk from 59th St-Columbus Circle station

See stage productions penned by some of today's most noteworthy wordsmiths at **Playwrights Horizons** (p103).
9min walk from Times Sq-42nd St station

Reach the top of the **Empire State Building** (p112), an emblem of NYC's art deco era.
2min walk from 34th St-Herald Sq station

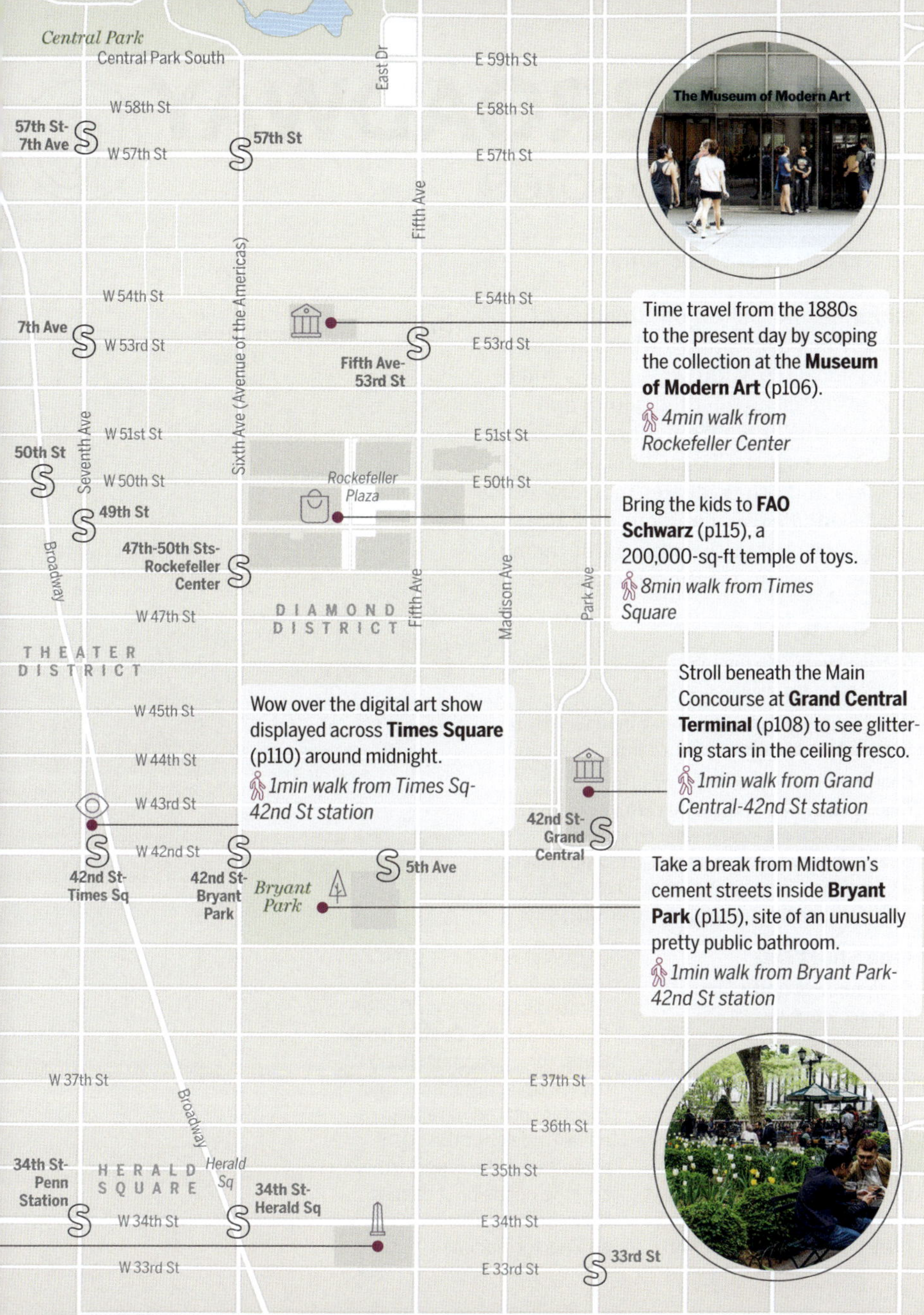

Central Park
Central Park South
East Dr
E 59th St
W 58th St
E 58th St
57th St-7th Ave
W 57th St
57th St
E 57th St
Fifth Ave
The Museum of Modern Art
W 54th St
E 54th St
Sixth Ave (Avenue of the Americas)
7th Ave
W 53rd St
Fifth Ave-53rd St
E 53rd St
Time travel from the 1880s to the present day by scoping the collection at the Museum of Modern Art (p106).
4min walk from Rockefeller Center
Seventh Ave
W 51st St
E 51st St
50th St
W 50th St
Rockefeller Plaza
E 50th St
49th St
Bring the kids to FAO Schwarz (p115), a 200,000-sq-ft temple of toys.
8min walk from Times Square
Broadway
47th-50th Sts-Rockefeller Center
W 47th St
DIAMOND DISTRICT
Fifth Ave
Madison Ave
Park Ave
THEATER DISTRICT
Stroll beneath the Main Concourse at Grand Central Terminal (p108) to see glittering stars in the ceiling fresco.
1min walk from Grand Central-42nd St station
W 45th St
Wow over the digital art show displayed across Times Square (p110) around midnight.
1min walk from Times Sq-42nd St station
W 44th St
W 43rd St
42nd St-Grand Central
W 42nd St
42nd St-Times Sq
42nd St-Bryant Park
Bryant Park
5th Ave
Take a break from Midtown's cement streets inside Bryant Park (p115), site of an unusually pretty public bathroom.
1min walk from Bryant Park-42nd St station
W 37th St
E 37th St
Broadway
E 36th St
34th St-Penn Station
HERALD SQUARE
Herald Sq
E 35th St
34th St-Herald Sq
W 34th St
E 34th St
W 33rd St
E 33rd St
33rd St

19 BROADWAY Babies

MUSICALS | MUSEUM | DINING

Seeing a show on Broadway: office work aside, that's what brings many locals to Midtown – unless you're one of the city's talented actors and singers who come from afar to make it on NYC's stages. Chorus kids, seasoned hoofers and other theater industry professionals live, hang out and, if lucky, perform in the area. Meet them at their favorite neighborhood spots.

How to

Getting there Take the subway to Times Sq-42nd St, center of the theater district.

When to go Plan a theater outing from Tuesday to Sunday. Monday is Broadway's day off.

Celebrate new works There are plenty of long-running Broadway classics that attract out-of-towners, but most local theater connoisseurs scratch their entertainment itch at recently opened productions. Check the *New York Times* and *New York Magazine* theater sections to see what's hot.

0 500 m
0 0.25 miles
W 54th St
54 Below
7th Ave
W 52nd St
Eighth Ave
Broadway
Sixth Ave (Avenue of the Americas)
W 50th St
50th St
50th St
49th St
THEATER DISTRICT
Ninth Ave
47th-50th Sts-Rockefeller Center
W 47th St
W 46th St
Joe Allen
Bar Centrale
TKTS Booth
W 45th St
Museum of Broadway
W 44th St
Sardi's
New Victory
Playwrights Horizons
W 43rd St
W 42nd St
42nd St-Port Authority
42nd St-Times Sq
42nd St-Bryant Park
Dyer St
Drama Book Shop
W 39th St
Seventh Ave
Broadway
GARMENT DISTRICT

One Short Day

Stage nerds unite Before running into New York's theater cognoscenti, brush up on your B'way knowledge. At the **Museum of Broadway**, you'll dance through three centuries of razzmatazz spread across four floors – including artifacts, costumes and props. Visitors also get a peek behind the curtain with an exhibit showcasing the making of a Broadway show.

After learning your Do-Re-Mi's, skip to the **Drama Book Shop** (dramabookshop.com) to pick up scripts and other theater-related paraphernalia. Check out the event calendar: writers, performers and the occasional casting director pop in for readings and performances.

Top right TKTS Booth
Bottom right Joe Allen

KATHY IMAGES/SHUTTERSTOCK ©

ANNE CZICHOS/SHUTTERSTOCK ©

Discount Tickets

You may experience sticker shock while purchasing Broadway tickets: some seats carry three-digit prices. Luckily, there are ways to see theater at a fraction of the cost. For the most options, visit **TKTS Booth** in Times Square, where you can get up to 50% off same-day shows and next-day matinees (lines can be long). Most shows also hold lotteries, allowing select winners to purchase choice seats at bargain prices. The TodayTix app offers discounted pricing in all forms, including digital lotteries.

Best Off-Broadway Plenty of non-Broadway theaters welcome the industry's biggest names. Off-Broadway company **Playwrights Horizons** produces some of New York's most innovative productions. If you've got kids in tow, check out the **New Victory** – a 42nd St theater for young audiences. Theater fans should also consider a cabaret and dinner at **54 Below**, where everyone from Tony Award winners to New York's up-and-coming stars belt the night away.

Cast party For a taste of old-school insider Broadway, stop by **Sardi's** – a restaurant with walls covered in caricatures of famous patrons. After curtain call, you might spot actors at **Bar Centrale** or **Joe Allen**, both on 46th St's Restaurant Row.

How Broadway Came to Be

FROM THOROUGHFARE TO THEATER

Broadway, the 13-mile road bisecting Manhattan, is more than a street. According to songwriters, it's where 'the neon lights are bright' and where you can 'listen to the lullaby.' It's also where audiences gather between 41st and 54th Sts, waiting with bated breath as curtains rise on first-rate stage craft. Give your regards.

Left Times Square **Centre** Street signs **Right** 42nd St theaters

DARRYL BROOKS/SHUTTERSTOCK ©

Broadway's Beginnings

Search the corner of 46th St and Broadway for the bronze figure of a cheery gentleman, his right hand resting on a cane as he stares adoringly over Times Square's throng. This is George M Cohan, New York's multi-hyphenate showman, perched upon a pedestal inscribed with a quote – 'Give my regards to Broadway.' The lyric, which he wrote for the 1904 musical comedy *Little Johnny Jones,* melodically cemented what in-the-know New Yorkers figured out long ago: the boulevard called Broadway was the epicenter of great American entertainment.

Over 250 years before, Dutch colonizers called the southern tip of this thoroughfare *Brede Wegh* (Broad Way) – a muddy trail trod by livestock on their way to graze grasses near present-day City Hall. When the British took over, they anglicized the street's name. Broad and Way harmoniously joined forces soon after.

In 1798, the Park Theater became the first major stage to open near Lower Manhattan's section of Broadway, its backside facing Theater Alley (the alley remains; the theater is gone). As the city expanded northward, artists followed, and by the 1860s most upper-crust stages clustered around bustling Broadway-crossed Union Square. Companies that strayed too far from Broadway couldn't hack it – unless they happened to be smaller, grittier spaces entertaining working-class masses around the Bowery. For anyone who wanted success in 'legitimate' theater, however, Broadway was the place to be.

The industry continued tap dancing uptown in subsequent years – until 1904, when NYC's Theater District took center stage around a new subway station: 42nd St and Broadway. The train line provided theaters with a steady supply of cus-

JUAN CARLOS ALONSO LOPEZ/SHUTTERSTOCK ©

BJANKA KADIC/ALAMY STOCK PHOTO ©

tomers, as did nearby Penn Station and Grand Central Terminal. Proscenium arches populated the area to meet demand, their marquees lighting the night with bright, white incandescent bulbs (hence Broadway's moniker 'Great White Way').

Oklahoma elevated the musical from frivolous comedy to serious drama and inspired generations of writers to come

Broadway Today

'Broadway' might seem like an anomaly – only a few Broadway houses actually line the street. But as NYC productions began touring the country in the 19th century, marketing a show as 'Direct from Broadway' carried prestige, promising the gold standard of great performances. The name stuck.

To be considered a Broadway production today, the show must play a Broadway theater – one of the 500-plus seat houses located in Midtown's Theater District. (Theaters with 100 to 499 seats are considered Off-Broadway.) Broadway as a descriptor, however, is often used interchangeably with one theatrical style: the musical.

The modern musical – which integrates music, dance and scripted dialogue – is an art form born out of revues and vaudeville, both popular in turn-of-the-century NYC. You can thank composer-and-lyricist team Rodgers and Hammerstein for the style beloved today. Their revolutionary script-and-score piece *Oklahoma* (1943) elevated the musical from frivolous comedy to serious drama and inspired generations of writers to come. Today's longest-running Broadway shows are stylistically similar – doused with *Oklahoma* earnestness and George M Cohan optimism. No wonder his Times Square statue looks pleased.

Stage-to-Screen NYC Musicals

West Side Story (2021) Stephen Spielberg's remake of this 1960s classic follows rival gangs from different ethnic backgrounds as they fight for space in a changing city.

In the Heights (2021) *Hamilton* composer Lin-Manuel Miranda's first musical dances through dreams of a tight-knit Washington Heights community.

On the Town (1949) Three sailors arrive in NYC for an action-packed 24 hours in the heart of Manhattan.

Annie (1982) A plucky orphan goes from rags to riches as the Great Depression rages in NYC.

Hair (1979) Long-haired hippies search for serenity amid social upheaval while protesting the Vietnam War.

20 MOMA'S Sculpture Garden

ART | NATURE | MUSEUM

Name a notable Western world artist from the 19th century onward – Van Gogh, Picasso, Warhol, Bourgeois – and the Museum of Modern Art probably shows their best work among its 200,000-piece collection. For aesthetes, it's an encounter with the sublime, but for the uninitiated, it can be overwhelming. Take a break from the cultural crash course by meditating in the museum's serene sculpture garden.

JEAN BROOKS / ALAMY STOCK PHOTO ©

How to

Getting here Take the B/D/F/M to 47th-50th Sts/Rockefeller Center.

When to go The museum is open from 10:30pm to 5:30pm every day but Friday, when it closes at 7pm.

Tickets Purchasing tickets online in advance is the only way to guarantee museum entry; you'll also save $2 per ticket. moma.org

Food The on-site **Bar Room's** à la carte menu and the **Modern's** prix fixe are both pricey. Opt instead for cafe fare on floors 2 and 6.

ARTYOORAN/SHUTTERSTOCK ©

STEFANO POLITI MARKOVINA/SHUTTERSTOCK ©

Top left Abby Aldrich Rockefeller Sculpture Garden **Bottom left** MoMA **Right** MoMA

Art Outdoors

Garden galavant The **Abby Aldrich Rockefeller Sculpture Garden** is a breath of fresh air on MoMa's 1st floor, breaking up Midtown's arboreal abstinence with weeping beech, Chinese elm and birch trees – the latter planted to complement the space's marble floor tiles. Designed by Philip Johnson in 1953 as a 'roofless room,' the garden begs visitors to pause. Grab a chair in whatever corner seems most attractive and admire a rotating selection of sculptures and seasonal flora, bursting with color between spring and autumn. Art isn't the only colorful thing on display: flower beds and leafy trees are favorites among urban birds. Look for the beige belly of a mourning dove, the tufted red coat of a cardinal, the bright yellow breast of a warbler and more fantastic outfits sported by avian visitors.

Meditation station If you've got headphones handy, turn this into a guided meditation. A recording of the museum's security department manager, Chet Gold, leads listeners through a brief breathing exercise created specifically for garden guests. Visit moma.org/audio/playlist/294/3861 to tune in.

Indoor alternatives Inclement weather doesn't dash hopes of finding calm amid MoMa's crowded galleries. If you're a cinephile, get cozy in an on-site **theater** – same-day tickets are free with admission; see moma.org/film. With kids in tow, drop by the **Heyman Family Art Lab**, where little ones play 'artist' for the day.

Mini Guide to Unmissable Art

Attempting to see everything in MoMA's 630,000-sq-ft space could take half a day or more – a surefire way to experience museum fatigue. Instead, go through the collection chronologically, ensuring to glimpse the big names on display. Work your way down: Floor 5 covers the 1880s–1940s. Count on seeing Van Gogh's swirling *Starry Night* and Monet's Impressionist water lilies. Floor 4 tackles the 1940s–1970s, with Jackson Pollock and Andy Warhol on display. Take time with Faith Ringgold's 1967 response to Picasso's *Guernica in American People Series #20: Die*. On floor 2, 1970s–present, there's Richard Serra's *Equal*, composed of 80-ton steel stacks.

21 See Stars in GRAND CENTRAL

ARCHITECTURE | FOOD | HISTORY

Don't rush through this beaux-arts station hall from 1913 like Metro North's commuters. Grand Central Terminal evokes railroad romance with its ornate interior designs. Most magical is its marble-trimmed concourse: gaze at the vaulted ceiling to see the night sky's glittering constellations. Spend at least an hour uncovering secrets within this architectural love letter to train travel's Golden Age.

OSCITY/SHUTTERSTOCK ©

How to

Getting here The 4/5/6, 7 and S trains all link to Grand Central. For a grand entrance, walk through the main doors at 89 East 42nd St, where you'll see the world's largest Tiffany-made clock.

When to go Avoid weekly morning and evening rush hours.

Dining Food and drink options here are exceptional. Try **Grand Central Market** (fast casual), **Oyster Bar & Restaurant** (fine dining), **Grand Central City Winery** and the **Campbell**, which features live jazz on weekend evenings.

MARCOBRIVIO.PHOTOGRAPHY/SHUTTERSTOCK ©

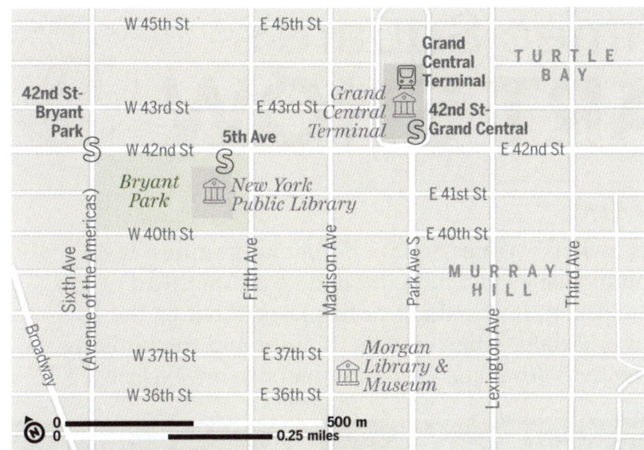

Train Station Tour

God's point of view Upon reaching the **Main Concourse**, stare up. The starry sky above isn't original – it's a 1944 copy covering water damage in the first fresco designed by French painter Paul Cesar Helleu. A 1990s renovation added twinkling lights (part of Helleu's original plan) and cleaned the ceiling. Follow Cancer's claws to the northwest corner to a tiny black rectangle: an unretouched patch of soot, approximately 9in by 5in, caused by decades of air pollutants. While admiring the work, examine the layout. The zodiac is actually backward. After its unveiling, railroad officials swatted critics away, saying it was painted from the perspective of God.

Acorns everywhere Look closely at the four-sided, opal glass clock atop the concourse's information kiosk (worth a cool $20 million) and notice its acorn cap. The Vanderbilt family funded the station's construction and wanted to ensure their mark was clear. The family's motto: 'From an acorn, a mighty oak shall grow.' Similar oak leaf-and-acorn stone motifs decorate the complex.

Acoustic quirk Head to the **Whispering Gallery** between the Main Concourse and Vanderbilt Hall to experience an auditory oddity. Stand corner-to-corner with a friend, ears pressed against the Guastavino tiles and carry on a conversation sotto voce. No one else will hear.

Bright lights Impressed by the chain-hanging chandeliers? There are 15, each containing 110 light bulbs and weighing around 1200lb.

Far left Main Concourse, Grand Central Terminal **Bottom left** Morgan Library & Museum

More Divine Ceilings

If your neck isn't sore from staring up at Grand Central Terminal, hop over to **New York Public Library** – the main branch of NYC's library system and the largest marble structure in the US upon completion in 1911. The Rose Reading Room, a two-block-long beauty with soaring ceilings covered in celestial murals, dazzles within. Free first-come, 15-minute room tours run at 11:20am, 1:30pm and 3pm Monday to Saturday. The nearby **Morgan Library & Museum** – a repository for Gilded Age steel magnate John Pierpoint Morgan's art-and-book collection – showcases more vaulted wonders dripping with Italian Renaissance splendor ($25 per adult).

22 Times Square's ART SHOW

NEON LIGHTS | BILLBOARDS | ART

There isn't a dimmer switch – Times Square perpetually shines. It's a splash of Vegas, a soupçon of Disney and a digital deluge of American commercialism. Love it or loathe it, it's hard not to be mesmerized by the lights – particularly around midnight, when crowds thin out and the blinking billboards momentarily transform from ads into an immersive art experience.

MICHAEL MULLER/SHUTTERSTOCK ©

How to

Getting here Times Square runs from 42nd St to 47th St between Broadway and Seventh Ave, accessible from the Times Square-42nd St station. Avoid taking cabs – traffic is a nightmare.

When to go The digital art show begins nightly at 11:57pm. Times Square is usually packed during the day – a place New Yorkers avoid, though fascinating to witness at least once in a lifetime.

Tip Avoid Times Square restaurants. Head to Ninth Ave in Hell's Kitchen, a neighborhood on Midtown's west side, for global eats.

RBLFMR/SHUTTERSTOCK ©

Top left Times Square
Bottom left Hell's Kitchen restaurant
Right Midnight Moment

Get Lost in Lights

From ads to art Facades are the faces of most New York neighborhoods, but here, it's all about the ads. Building exteriors have been transformed into de facto canvases for products, and many feature electronic billboards that run videos around the clock – except from 11:57pm to midnight, when **Midnight Moment** turns Times Square into the world's largest digital public-art program.

The show, running since 2012, synchronizes 92 digital displays between 41st and 49th St for a three-minute, immersive contemporary art spectacle. Works change monthly, featuring well-known names like Andy Warhol and contemporary boundary-breakers in the digital-art ecosystem. For the most mesmerizing view, climb the 27 red steps above the TKTS Booth at 47th St and watch art appear all around.

From peep shows to people If you told a New Yorker that Times Square would become a coveted place to showcase art 30 years ago, they would've laughed. Starting in the 1960s, Times Square became a pit for peep shows, porn theaters and three-card monte scammers; in 1981, *Rolling Stone* dubbed 42nd St the 'sleaziest block in America.' All that changed in the mid-1990s when city mandates downgraded the area's X-rating to a G (the contentious Naked Cowboy not included). Now, roughly 360,000 people pass through Times Square each day. Luckily, crowds often thin out by midnight; the area is most packed during daylight hours.

Naming the Square

Making money is central to Times Square's identity. Before its current name, the area was called Longacre Sq. Then, when the IRT (NYC's first subway line) announced a Longacre subway station in 1904, businesses began speculating a move nearby could increase profits. This included the *New York Times,* which decided to move to Broadway and 42nd St the same year. The decision was genius: with an 'in-house' subway station, the newspaper earned faster distribution and increased commuter sales. Cherry on top? The square was renamed in its honor. The *Times* moved west in 1913, but one of its traditions remains – ringing in the new year.

23 The Empire State BUILDING

PANORAMAS | SKYSCRAPERS | CITY LIGHTS

There's a reason King Kong chose this skyscraper above the rest. One World Trade Center might be taller and the Chrysler Building might be prettier, but when it comes to skyline landmarks, the Empire State Building (ESB) is NYC's queen. Take the vertiginous elevator ride to the top of this urban icon for spectacular city views that shift with the sun.

ASHFAQ KARIM/SHUTTERSTOCK ©

How to

Getting here The ESB is a five-minute walk from the 34th St subway stations at Herald Square and Penn Station.

When to go If opting for the outdoor sky deck, visit between spring and autumn for pleasant temperatures.

Tickets Prices start at $44/38 adult/child. Opening hours change seasonally. Visit esbnyc.com to reserve timed tickets.

Grab a bite For an inexpensive, tasty bite inside the building, stop by **Tacombi**, a city chain serving Baja-inspired tacos and burritos.

ANDRISK/SHUTTERSTOCK ©

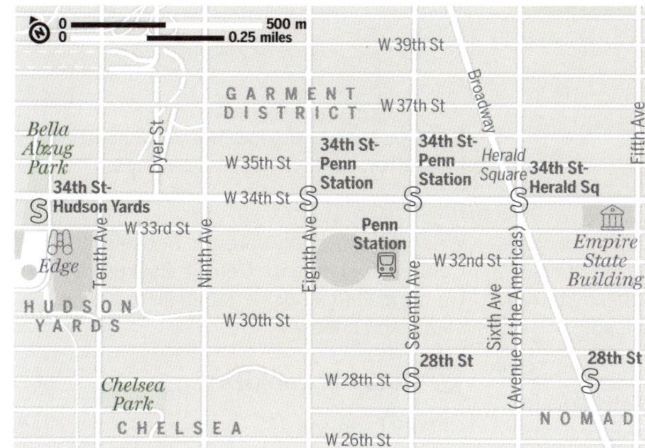

Top left Empire State Building
Bottom left 86th floor observation deck

Sunrise to Sunset

Choose your time Sunset is the most beautiful time to visit, just as Manhattan's skyscrapers morph into glittering nightlights, but you'll have to pay a $10 surcharge. If you're an early riser, try the Sunrise Experience, which jolts visitors awake with a 5:45am arrival time on Saturdays ($135). The tour includes plenty of coffee and few other visitors, making this ideal for beating crowds. If you hate mornings, crowds and extra fees, consider visiting between noon and 2pm once the day's first rush is over and the masses thin out.

Stay up late Visit after dark and get front-row seats to a serious light show. The ESB's top 30 floors light up with LEDs capable of displaying over 16 million colors. They're usually white but turn kaleidoscopic to celebrate things like holidays, local sports teams and charitable organizations.

Choose your view There are two observation decks: the 86th floor, which is outdoors, and a tiny round room with floor-to-ceiling windows on the 102nd floor. The 102nd floor costs an additional $35, so it's fair to say the 86th is plenty satisfying.

Beyond the deck Admission grants access to exhibitions on the 2nd and 80th floors, which include history about the ESB's construction and its place in pop culture. Don't miss the photo-op with King Kong's giant paw.

Head Above the Rest

Built in a frenzied 410 days, this steel-framed, limestone-and-granite-clad art deco emblem opened in 1931 with a spectacular title – the world's tallest building. Its 103 floors stretch 1250 vertical feet, with an antenna bringing its height to 1454ft top to bottom. ESB held the title for 40 years – until the World Trade Center's Twin Towers climbed 100ft higher. Other Midtown observation decks also vie for attention, including the **Edge** at Hudson Yards – the western hemisphere's highest outdoor observation deck – where you can don a helmet and harness to climb outside for the highest open-air building ascent in the world ($185).

Listings

BEST OF THE REST

Fine-Dining Favorites

Le Bernardin $$$

French-born chef Eric Ripert has spent decades steering this restaurant to deceptively simple seafood heaven. It's the triple-Michelin-starred holy grail of gills. Book a month ahead.

Monkey Bar $$$

The reasons to drop serious dough here are plenty: there's the giant Jazz Age mural, the extensive steakhouse menu, a cocktail list to match – and it's been around since 1937.

Asian Eats

LumLum $$

Throw a dart in Hell's Kitchen and you'll hit a Thai restaurant – just try hitting this beach-themed spot first. Bamboo walls, tropical art – it's no secret that fish is the specialty.

Urban Hawker $$

Stalls specializing in Singaporean street food crackle with treats like Hainanese chicken rice (poached, roasted or fried), best served by **Hainan Jones** – a favorite among Midtown's office workers at lunchtime.

HanGawi $$$

Vegetarians, take note. There are plenty of meat-forward, fish-sauced restaurants in Koreatown (around 32nd St between Madison and Sixth Aves), but only one shoe-free, floor-cushioned spot serving delectable veggie fare.

Bakeries & Pizza Shops

Amy's Bread $

Amy started buttering up Hell's Kitchen in 1992; she now sells sweets all over the city. Pop into this cheery location to taste her baguettes, sandwiches and pastries.

Ace's Pizza $

When hunger strikes around Rockefeller Center, head here for Detroit-style pizza slices (rectangular clouds of dough slathered in sauce and cheese).

Coffee & Cookies

Culture Espresso $

Don't be fooled by the name. Though the coffee is some of Midtown's best, you're coming here for uber-gooey cookies so good they rival city favorite Levain.

Remi43 Flower & Coffee $

Feeling fatigued from pounding the gray pavement? Recharge inside this petal-packed florist shop-cum-cafe, where the latte art is as picture-worthy as the plants.

Sceney Spots for Drinks

Pebble Bar $$$

With its roster of celebrity investors, this townhouse bar has done the unthinkable –

Rudy's Bar & Grill

created a Rockefeller Center cocktail scene that's actually cool. Drinks are expensive ($21), but the atmosphere can't be beat.

Tomi Jazz $$

Stumble down to this Japanese jazz den after 6pm, when whiskey flows as freely as an improvised sax solo. It's hard to believe this isn't the East Village.

Beer & Dive Bars

As Is $$

Hell's Kitchen's beer heads agree – this hops den is tops. Sample some of the 20 beers on tap while sitting by the big 10th Ave-facing windows. Don't skimp on the pub grub.

Rudy's Bar & Grill $

The big pants-free pig outside should have told you – this is Hell's Kitchen's best dive, with cheap pitchers of beer, vinyl booths patched with duct tape and free hot dogs.

Toys & Trains

FAO Schwarz

Claiming to be America's oldest toy store (opened in 1862 and synonymous with NYC since 1870), this kid's bazaar is certainly grand. It includes the giant floor piano from *Big*.

New York Transit Museum Store

On Grand Central Terminal's east side, next to the stationmaster's office, you'll find this outpost of Brooklyn's New York Transit Museum – a nifty shop and gallery with transit-themed swag.

Haberdashery & Homewares

Fine & Dandy

Dapper folks drop into this pocket-square-sized haberdashery for retro fashion accessories: hats, bow ties, ascots, embroidered suspenders, cufflinks and even spats.

Delphinium Home

Super cute, a little quirky and a lot of fun: this is Hell's Kitchen's go-to for greeting cards, candles, home furnishings and kitschy gifts fit for just about everyone.

Museums & Public Spaces

United Nations

Enter international territory at this mid-century modern complex designed by Le Corbusier and Oscar Niemeyer, peeking inside the UN's hallowed headquarters on an hour-long tour. Prebooking and government-issued ID required.

Intrepid Sea, Air & Space Museum

This hulking aircraft carrier floating in the Hudson survived a WWII bomb and kamikaze attacks. Today it houses an interactive military museum with videos, historical artifacts and frozen-in-time living quarters.

Bryant Park

European coffee kiosks, alfresco chess games and seasonal outdoor events for the whole family: this leafy Parisian-style park is a whimsical break from Midtown's mayhem. In December there's a holiday market.

Rockefeller Center

Midtown's 22-acre art deco emblem was envisioned as a 'city within a city' during its Great Depression–era construction. The final product succeeded: theaters, restaurants, a skating rink and views from the Top of the Rock observation deck keep it perpetually abuzz.

UPPER EAST SIDE

MUSEUMS | TRADITIONS | AESTHETHES

UPPER EAST SIDE

Trip Builder

TAKE YOUR PICK OF MUST-SEES AND HIDDEN GEMS

The Upper East Side (UES) radiates elegance from Central Park all the way down to the East River. Mansion-stacked Fifth Ave is designated 'Museum Mile' from 82nd St to the top of the park; blue bloods reign supreme until Third Ave; and Second Ave is for laid-back pubs and grub.

Neighborhood Notes

Best for Magnificent museums and gilded grandeur.

Transportation 4/5/6 along Lexington Ave; N/Q/R along Second Ave. Crosstown buses at 66th, 72nd, 79th, 86th and 96th Sts.

Getting around Plan on walking.

Tip Fifth Ave borders Central Park's Jacqueline Kennedy Onassis Reservoir at 90th St – a scenic spot for strolling.

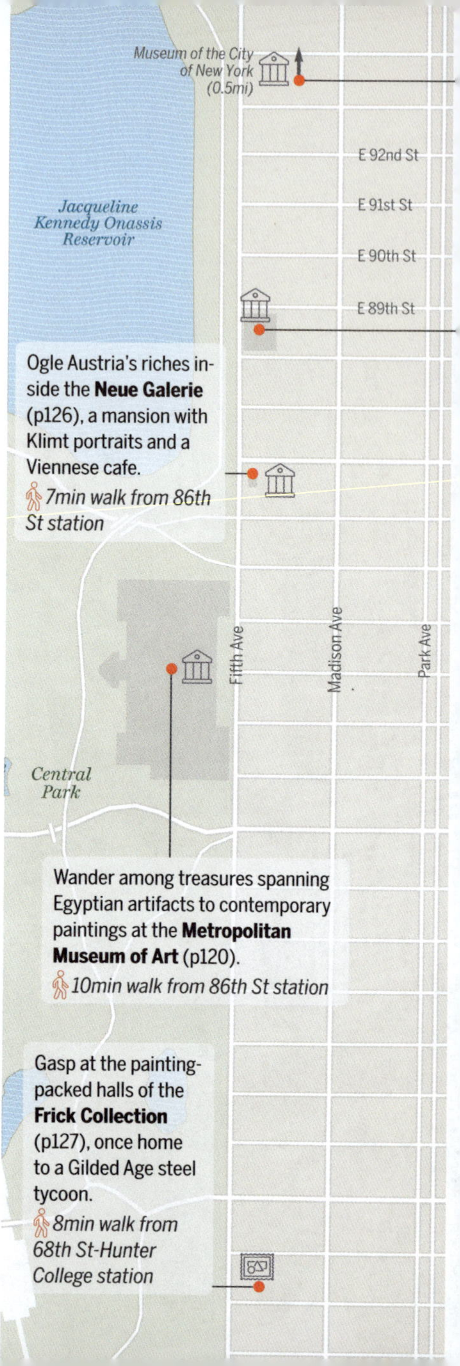
Museum of the City of New York (0.5mi)
E 92nd St
E 91st St
E 90th St
E 89th St
Jacqueline Kennedy Onassis Reservoir
Ogle Austria's riches inside the **Neue Galerie** (p126), a mansion with Klimt portraits and a Viennese cafe.
7min walk from 86th St station
Fifth Ave
Madison Ave
Park Ave
Central Park
Wander among treasures spanning Egyptian artifacts to contemporary paintings at the **Metropolitan Museum of Art** (p120).
10min walk from 86th St station
Gasp at the painting-packed halls of the **Frick Collection** (p127), once home to a Gilded Age steel tycoon.
8min walk from 68th St-Hunter College station

Travel through 400 years of local history at the **Museum of the City of New York** (p131).
8min walk from 103rd St station

Walk up Frank Lloyd Wright's architectural coil at the **Solomon R Guggenheim Museum** (p131).
4min walk from the Neue Galerie

Order sausages from **Schaller & Weber** (p130), one of a few remaining businesses from Yorkville's German heyday.
1min walk from 86th St Q station

Sip an egg cream at **Lexington Candy Shop** (p124), New York's oldest family-run luncheonette.
4min walk from 86th St station

Escape to **Roosevelt Island** (p128) for panoramic views and traffic so light it feels like leaving NYC.
4min tram ride from 60th St and Second Ave

Munch on burgers and down martinis at old-school UES favorite **JG Melon** (p125).
5min walk from 77th St station

Head upstairs to **2nd Floor Bar & Essen** (p131), a shtetl-style speakeasy above a kosher deli.
7min walk from 72nd St Q station

24 Treasure Hunt at THE MET

PAINTINGS | STATUES | ARCHITECTURE

The palatial Metropolitan Museum of Art, founded in 1870, is a bastion of world-class art, celebrating 5000 years of human creativity with one-million-plus objects spanning the globe. Conquering it all in a day is impossible; instead, explore a small collection of its most magnificent artifacts and galleries.

BRIAN LOGAN PHOTOGRAPHY /SHUTTERSTOCK ©

How to

Getting here Take the 4/5/6 to 86th St and walk half a mile west.

When to go Midday is busiest: arrive at opening or a couple of hours before closing to avoid congestion.

Crowd Control The Great Hall entrance looks magnificent, but you'll beat crowds by joining the entry line at 81st St. Pre-book tickets online at metmuseum.org.

Dining There are cafes throughout, but eat before arriving. Food here is subpar and pricey.

ARCOBRIVIO.PHOTOGRAPHY/SHUTTERSTOCK ©

SERGE YATUNIN/SHUTTERSTOCK ©

Egyptian Art

Start by skipping through Egyptian history in 39 galleries covering the Paleolithic to Roman eras (c 300,000 BCE to 400 CE). The must-see piece here is the **Temple of Dendur** (Gallery 131). It's the only complete Egyptian temple on display in the Western Hemisphere, built over 2000 years ago on the banks of the Nile. After admiring the craftsmanship, stop by Gallery 136 to meet William, a blue faience (glazed earthenware) hippopotamus with an essential museum job: Met mascot. Discovered in a tomb in 1910 and acquired by the Met in 1917, the hippo quickly became the museum's quirky frontman, earning his name from a British humor magazine.

Greek & Roman Art

With over 30,000 individual pieces, this is North America's most comprehensive

Met Must-Dos

Use the Met's free audio guide – an exceptional resource available on your smartphone (metmuseum.org/audio-guide).

Check the Met's website for free docent-led tours to specific galleries.

Sign up for temporary exhibits by joining the virtual queue via QR code at the entrance – they're usually worthwhile.

Top left Metropolitan Museum of Art
Bottom left Renaissance Revival Room
Above Temple of Dendur

assemblage of toga-wearing trophies. It's easy to get stuck gaping at chiseled gods in the Great Hall, but head instead to the sunlit **Leon Levy & Shelby White Roman Sculpture Court** (Gallery 162). Bonus points for spotting the headless Three Graces of Greek mythology – Beauty, Mirth and Abundance – and the marble statue of a bearded Hercules.

European Paintings

From Giotto to Gauguin, the Met has it all: religious iconography from the 13th century, every Dutch master you can name and a sweeping selection of 19th-century French Impressionists. The dozen-plus paintings in the Vincent van Gogh collection is particularly captivating – and unlike his *Starry Night* at MoMA, you won't have to tussle with swarms to see his work. Stand before his *White Field with Cypresses* (Gallery 822) to imagine a blustery day in Saint-Rémy-de-Provence, then stare into his melancholy eyes at *Self Portrait with a Straw Hat* (Gallery 825).

Events & Further Exploration

Date Night at the Met
On weekends the Met gets romantic with live music. Bring someone special for drinks in the American Wing Cafe and Petrie Court Cafe, 5pm to 9pm Friday and Saturday.

Met Expert Talks Curators, scientists and scholars regularly lead in-depth, 30- to 45-minute explorations of objects within a particular gallery. Check the Met's schedule and register for a spot.

Met fashion exhibit Every May, celebrities dress in various fashions related to a theme for the Met Gala. This coincides with the opening of the Costume Institute's spring fashion exhibit, showcasing a collection of theme-related designs. The show runs through summer – always a hit.

ITZAVU/SHUTTERSTOCK ©

Far left Leon Levy & Shelby White Roman Sculpture Court **Left** Charles Engelhard Court **Below** Cantor Roof Garden Bar

American Wing & Modern Art

The two-floor collection of American art decorating the museum's northwest corner covers everything from colonial times to the early 20th century, including Emanuel Luetze's iconic *Washington Crossing the Delaware,* which looms large over Gallery 760. If you need a pick-me-up, stop by the American Wing Cafe in the **Charles Engelhard Court** – a glass garden filled with American-made sculptures and framed by a marble facade that once graced Wall St.

Follow the American wing with modern and contemporary art in southwestern galleries, highlighting art-world titans from the late 19th century onward. Spend some time with Thomas Hart Benton's *America Today* (Gallery 909), a room-sized mural depicting the US at the Great Depression's onset.

Cantor Roof Garden Bar

If museum fatigue sets in, clear your head by floating above Central Park's trees. Art installations grace this **outdoor space**, and there's an unobstructed view of Midtown. Plan your visit around sunset on Friday and Saturday, when the sky improvises a painting that competes with the artwork. Enjoy the scene while sipping a cocktail.

PIT STOCK/SHUTTERSTOCK ©

MARCOBRIVIO.PHOTOGRAPHY/SHUTTERSTOCK ©

Time Hop at Lexington Candy Shop

NEW YORK'S OLDEST FAMILY-RUN LUNCHEONETTE

There's no shortage of expensive fine dining in NYC, especially around the tony Upper East Side. Amid its competitive restaurant scene, Lexington Candy Shop stands apart from the crowd. As new restaurants arrive, tempting customers with newfangled foods, this inexpensive holdout sticks to tradition – and its time-honored style remains unmatchable.

Left Lexington Candy Shop **Centre** Vintage Coca-Cola bottles **Right** Pastrami Queen

New York Time Capsule

In 1921 Greek immigrant Soterios Philis arrived in New York City and began saving money to open his own business. His dream came to fruition in 1925 when he stepped into this tiny corner shop three blocks from the Met – now, arguably, a museum-worthy piece in its own right. Deep-green booths, terrazzo floors and swivel stools look like a set for a Hollywood soda-shop flick. Vintage Coca-Cola bottles decorate windows lit up with neon signage. The mixer for shakes actually dates to 1948. This isn't the kind of place where you simply come for food (though it's all deliberately made with care and is delicious) – it's the kind of place you visit to time travel. New luncheonettes have sprouted up in recent years (Old John's on the Upper West Side; S&P in Midtown), attempting to capitalize on lunch-counter nostalgia, but there's no way to fabricate what makes this spot special: an entire century of commitment to excellence.

On the Menu

The name 'Candy Shop' might be misleading for the luncheonette today, but in 1925, Philis used the basement for whipping up chocolates. By 1948, he decided it wasn't worth the labor and focused instead on the business upstairs. Since then, the restaurant has been seemingly preserved in amber. You can still order all the same mid-century classics: milkshakes (vanilla, chocolate, strawberry and coffee), tuna melts, grilled cheese and even a peanut butter-and-jelly sandwich. For a taste of old-school New York, slurp down an egg cream (an NYC invention), which, like the luncheonette's name, is a misnomer – there's no egg and no cream in this chocolate-syrup soda,

SHAREALIKE/FLICKR/BY-NC-SA 2.0 ©

ROBERT K CHIN - STOREFRONTS/ALAMY STOCK PHOTO ©

served here in a tall glass with house-made syrup, seltzer and half-and-half.

John Philis, the third-generation owner, ensures his family's business maintains consistency. Juices are still freshly squeezed and the recipes remain untouched. The breads come from Orwashers Bakery (p130), open since 1916. The coffee comes from Queens-based Vassilaros & Sons, open since 1919. If you get a scoop of ice cream (or possibly a banana split), it's from Bassetts in Philadelphia – going strong since 1861.

> You can still order all the same mid-century classics: milkshakes, tuna melts, grilled cheese and even a peanut butter-and-jelly sandwich.

Triumph of the Oldie

There's nothing secret about this spot. Look at the walls and you'll see autographs of celebrities who've stopped by over the years and faded posters from movies that used it as a set piece (*Three Days of the Condor*, *Fading Gigolo* and *The Nanny Diaries*). TVs and commercials have been shot here, too, their production designers amorous for UES authenticity.

In a city known for reinvention, Lexington Candy Shop makes a strong argument for preservation. Around 80% of NYC restaurants close within five years, which means the Philis clan clearly has something figured out. Perhaps it's that the luncheonette closes reliably at 6pm, ensuring workers leave at a reasonable hour. Maybe it's the price point – always affordable. It could also be the service – relaxed, familial. Or perhaps a city filled with luncheonettes would never work. Perhaps what makes Lexington Candy Shop remarkable is that it's one-of-a-kind.

More Classic UES Bites

William Greenberg Desserts They started churning out kosher baked goods here in 1946. Come for rugelach (a tiny dough ball rolled with chocolate, jam and other sweet pastes) and the famous black-and-white cookie. Usually the size of a palm, you can order minis here.

JG Melon A no-frills pub that's been serving one of NYC's best burgers since 1972. Flushing down the beefcake with a Bloody Mary is a local rite of passage.

Pastrami Queen This place got its start in 1956 as 'Pastrami King.' The gender change only made this kosher deli more regal. Try her namesake sandwich, stacked skyscraper-high with beef, for proof.

25 Visit Austria at the NEUE GALERIE

ART | CAFE | MANSION

Stepping inside the Neue Galerie is like taking a first-class ticket to turn-of-the-century Austria. Once the mansion of a Vanderbilt, this jewel-box museum now showcases Austrian and German art from 1890 to 1940 alongside a restaurant with Viennese vim. Between gold-leaf Klimt portraits and bowls of goulash, you might think you're hanging with the Habsburgs.

How to

Getting here Take the 4/5 to 86th St and walk 10 minutes west.

When to go The museum is open 11am to 6pm Wednesday to Sunday. On the First Friday of every month, admission is free from 5pm to 8pm. Admission is first-come, first-served.

Shop smart Browse the connected bookstore – a museum unto itself, with artist monographs and coffee-table tomes.

Get a table Cafe Sabarsky doesn't take breakfast or lunch reservations, but you can book for dinner.

A gilded entrance Before transporting yourself to Austria, take a moment to delight in the beaux-arts exterior. Designed by Carrère and Hastings (architects behind New York Public Library) and completed in 1914, the mansion belongs to what was once called 'Millionaires' Row.' This stretch of Fifth Ave, skirting Central Park, became the Gilded Age home of New York's wealthiest residents.

A golden trophy Once inside, run your hand along the wrought-iron banister while winding up a central staircase to the 2nd floor. German Expressionist and Bauhaus artists are well represented in the collection, along with

Top right Neue Galerie
Bottom right Cafe Sabarsky

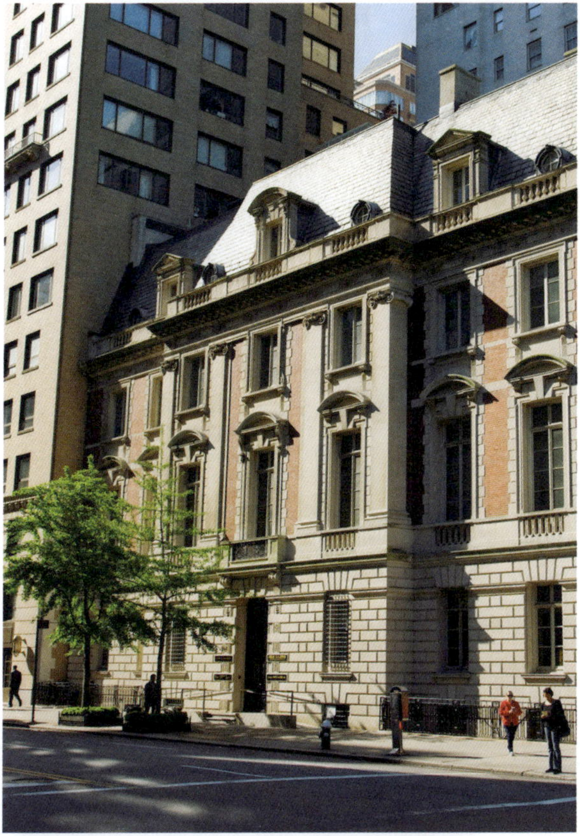

IMAGE PROFESSIONALS GMBH/ALAMY STOCK PHOTO ©

HEMIS/ALAMY STOCK PHOTO ©

More Gilded Age Mansions

Skip up Fifth Ave to admire more stately abodes transformed into museums. Most magnificent is the **Frick Collection**, another Carrère and Hastings design completed in 1914. The museum, which showcases Western European master painters, is worth a peep. There's also the **Cooper-Hewitt Smithsonian Design Museum**, constructed in 1902. Andrew Carnegie, the mansion's original owner, told his architects he wanted 'the most modest, plainest' home in New York. Enter the garden to consider if they answered his brief.

turn-of-the-20th-century Austrian creatives. As for the museum's most prized piece, that's Gustav Klimt's gold-flecked 1907 *Portrait of Adele Bloch-Bauer 1,* acquired for a whopping $135 million by cosmetics magnate and museum founder Ronald Lauder.

A gemütlich restaurant For a fully immersive experience, grab a table at **Cafe Sabarsky** – a Vienna-style coffee house within the mansion, designed to mimic classic Austrian cafes popular around the time of the home's construction. With dishes like bratwurst and *Topfentorte* (quark cheesecake), you might start thinking the Upper East Side is Europe's Eastern Alps.

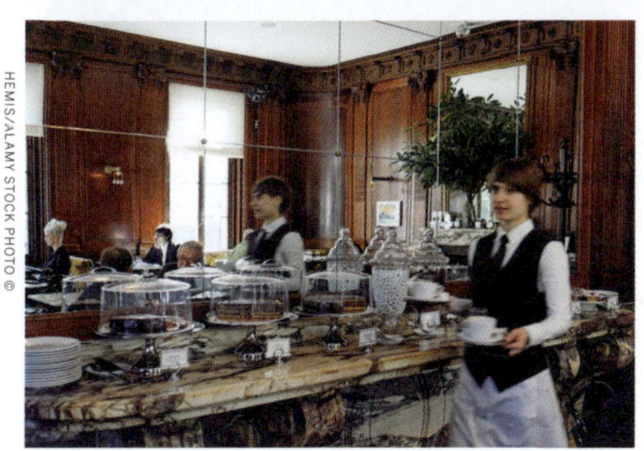

26 Take the Tram to ROOSEVELT ISLAND

VISTAS | MONUMENTS | PARKS

Hop on the cherry-red tramway at Second Ave and 60th St, and after a 4-minute flight, you're surrounded by small-town splendor. Most New Yorkers skip over this skinny 2-mile-long island between the Upper East Side and Queens, but the 14,000 New Yorkers who live here understand its charms. Savor captivating views while enjoying life in the slow lane.

How to

Getting here/around The F train stops at Roosevelt Island, but the tram is more magical and costs the same as a subway ride. Upon arrival, plan on walking. For an alternative to walking, hop on the free Red Bus looping the island.

When to go Visit for a late afternoon park stroll and early evening Panorama Room cocktail.

Consider cycling Wide lanes and little traffic make this a great place to bike; there's a Citi Bike station near the tram.

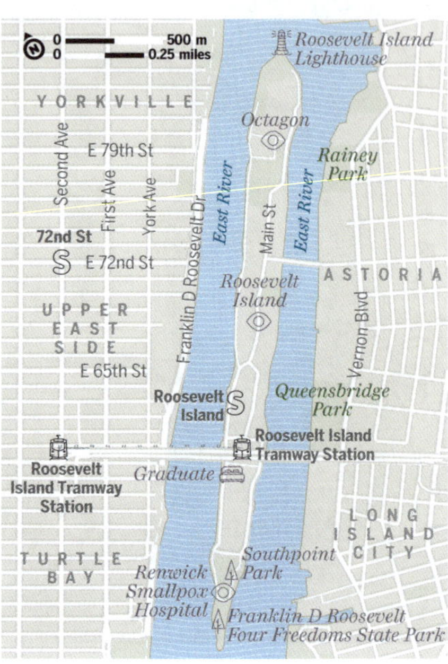

Island Adventure

Ride the tram Once you board, choose your view: stand on the right to see the beaux arts, cream-colored Queensboro Bridge (built in 1901) or the left to glimpse towers along the Upper East Side.

Visit the park Upon arrival, head south past the Cornell Tech campus toward **Franklin D Roosevelt Four Freedoms State Park**, where an allée of trees shoot above a triangular patch of grass and granite. The park's name comes from a famous Roosevelt address in 1941, outlining his vision for a world founded on four human freedoms: freedom of speech and expression, and freedom from want and fear. Look

Top right Roosevelt Island tram
Bottom right Franklin D Roosevelt Four Freedoms State Park

AGSAZ/SHUTTERSTOCK ©

STUDIO BCNOBO TOSHIO S/SHUTTERSTOCK ©

Island Asylum

Look beyond the area's university-chic aesthetic to uncover a turbulent past. In the 19th century, this was an asylum depot known as Blackwell's Island – a dumping ground for poor, sick, disabled and incarcerated locals. Largely abandoned in the 1950s, a few relics remain. In **Southpoint Park**, check out the ruins of the **Renwick Smallpox Hospital**. A 10-minute walk south from the **Gothic Revival lighthouse** leads to the **Octagon**, a lux apartment complex occupying the once-notorious New York Lunatic Asylum.

southwest and you'll spot a glass curtain democratically decorating the United Nations facade. Roosevelt's desire for global cooperation helped form the UN, established six months after his death in 1945. Look east to see a ruby-red Pepsi-Cola sign, decorating Long Island City's waterfront since 1936.

Soak in the view If you like the park's scenery, wait until you reach the **Panorama Room**, an 18th-floor cocktail lounge inside the **Graduate** hotel. Floor-to-ceiling windows overlook Manhattan, Queens, Brooklyn and the East River. If you get hungry, try the hotel's American-style restaurant, **Anything at All**, named for a quote from *The Great Gatsby*.

Listings

BEST OF THE REST

German Staples

Heidelberg $$

This German stalwart is one of the few survivors of a time when 86th St was called 'Sauerkraut Boulevard,' serving Bavarian beer and *Schweinshaxe* (pork shank) since 1936.

Schaller & Weber $$

A holdover from Yorkville's German enclave days, come here for sausages, imported European goodies and Schaller's Stube Sausage Bar next door, serving franks on buns (veggie options available).

Haute Cuisine

Tanoshi Sushi Sake Bar $$$

Guests pack in tighter than a hand roll for an unforgettable *omakase* (chef's choice) experience in a pocket-sized sushi spot with chef-facing seats. BYO beer, sake or whatnot.

Daniel $$$

You could splurge on the tasting menu, but sitting in the mahogany lounge to order à la carte is the best way to enjoy star chef Daniel Boulud's eponymous French restaurant.

Mission Ceviche $$$

Date night tip: drinking the Peruvian *leche de tigre* (ceviche juice) is supposedly an aphrodisiac – and most of these seafood-forward Peruvian plates come bathed in the magical tiger's milk.

Food with Global Flare

Drunken Munkey $$

Vintage wallpaper and cricket-ball door hangers might serve colonial Bombay pastiche, but the rich curries are the real deal. Expect plenty of spice; wash it down with a gin-based cocktail.

Migrant Kitchen $

The affordable, filling food at this philanthropically focused mini-chain makes American meals inspired by immigrants. Forget the hamburgers: it's all about cauliflower shawarma wraps and chorizo bowls here.

Vietnaam $

Stop by this modest Vietnamese spot for delicious dumplings, pho and bánh mì that won't break the bank.

Coffee & Sweets

Variety Coffee Roasters $

Smooth brews, delectable pastries and floor-to-ceiling windows that brighten the wood-slatted interior. No wonder the work-from-coffee-shop crowd fills up the UES outlet of this Brooklyn chain.

Orwashers Bakery $

Hungarian immigrants opened this bakery in 1916, which has been serving rye, black and grain breads ever since. Order yourself something sweet, like the sticky-bun babka or cherry cheese strudel.

Beer Halls & Gastropubs

Pony Bar $

If you're searching for a locally devout hop-topia around the UES, look no further than this craft-beer destination committed to American crafts, focusing on New York breweries.

Jeffrey $$

Post-work hops pursuers come to this unpretentious craft beer and cocktail bar under the Roosevelt Island tramway to choose from over 30 rotating taps.

Penrose $$

This Second Ave gastropub is famous for dirty pickle martinis, beer-battered pickles and its whiskey collection. It's also stylish, with exposed brick walls, vintage mirrors, reclaimed wood and experienced bartenders.

Go-Go Dancers & Games

Ethyl's Alcohol & Food $$

Burlesque shows, go-go dancers and music from the '60s and '70s make this bar a funky departure from the Upper East Side's stately side.

Hex & Co $$

Board games and beer go hand-in-hand at this cafe, which skews more 'mom's basement' than 'happening bar.' Choose from roughly 1000 games ($10 per player) and order some greasy feel-good grub.

Transportive Cocktails

2nd Floor Bar & Essen $$

The dimly lit staircase to this 2nd-floor annex is the portal to a 1920s speakeasy. Down creative drinks and shtetl-style bar bites inspired by the kosher deli below.

Auction House $$

Fat divans, gilded mirrors and hardwood floors: try enough of their cocktails, and you may wonder if it's the Victorian era.

Fantastic Museums & Performance Spaces

Museum of the City of New York

Exceptional pay-what-you-wish exhibits artfully illustrate the stories about this ever-evolving city. If you do one thing, spare 28 minutes for *Timescapes*, a multiscreen documentary chronicling 400 years of NYC history.

Solomon R Guggenheim Museum

Architect Frank Lloyd Wright's iconic inverted ziggurat spirals up from Fifth Ave like a steady crescendo. Expect the concrete coil to overshadow the rotating modern and contemporary artwork inside.

Jewish Museum

You might see this French Gothic chateau from 1908 and think the collection inside can't compete – but it does. The 30,000-piece collection explores 4000 years of Jewish art and culture.

Park Avenue Armory

Originally built for the Seventh Regiment of the National Guard in the 19th century, this Gothic Revival museum and theater turned its 55,000-sq-ft drill hall into one of NYC's largest stage spaces.

Unique Shops

SHOP Cooper Hewitt

New and established designers provide quirky home goods and decor monographs in this museum-affiliated shop inside Andrew Carnegie's former mansion.

Tiny Doll House

Obsessed with Carrie Stettheimer's dollhouse at the Museum of the City of New York? The tiny worlds here (Victorian, Chippendale, contemporary), rendered in stunning detail, will leave you speechless.

UPPER
WEST SIDE
HISTORIC | CULTURED | SERENE

UPPER WEST SIDE
Trip Builder

TAKE YOUR PICK OF MUST-SEES AND HIDDEN GEMS

The Upper West Side is a slice of old-school New York sandwiched between Central Park and the Hudson River. Feast your eyes on lavish prewar apartment buildings, fill your culture cup at landmarks like Lincoln Center, then devour museums both massive and miniature before unwinding in tranquil green spaces.

Neighborhood Notes

Best for Manicured parks, performing arts and architecture.

Transportation 1/2/3, B/C between Columbus Circle and 110th St stations. The A and D skip from Columbus Circle to Harlem.

Getting around Explore on foot or bike.

Tip Escape corporate mega-stores on Broadway for boutique shops and local eateries on Amsterdam and Columbus.

Wander through the free-to-visit **Nicholas Roerich Museum** (p145), a hidden town-house packed with vibrant paintings.
6min walk from 110th St station

Mosey along the spacious tree-lined promenade in **Riverside Park** (p140).
5min walk from 72nd St station

Shop for vintage threads and antique curios at the **Grand Bazaar NYC** (p145).
8min walk from 72nd St station

Stroll streets numbered in the 70s and 80s to pine over prewar architecture like the **Dakota Building** (p137).
1min walk from 72nd St station

Hudson River

0 500 m
0 0.25 miles

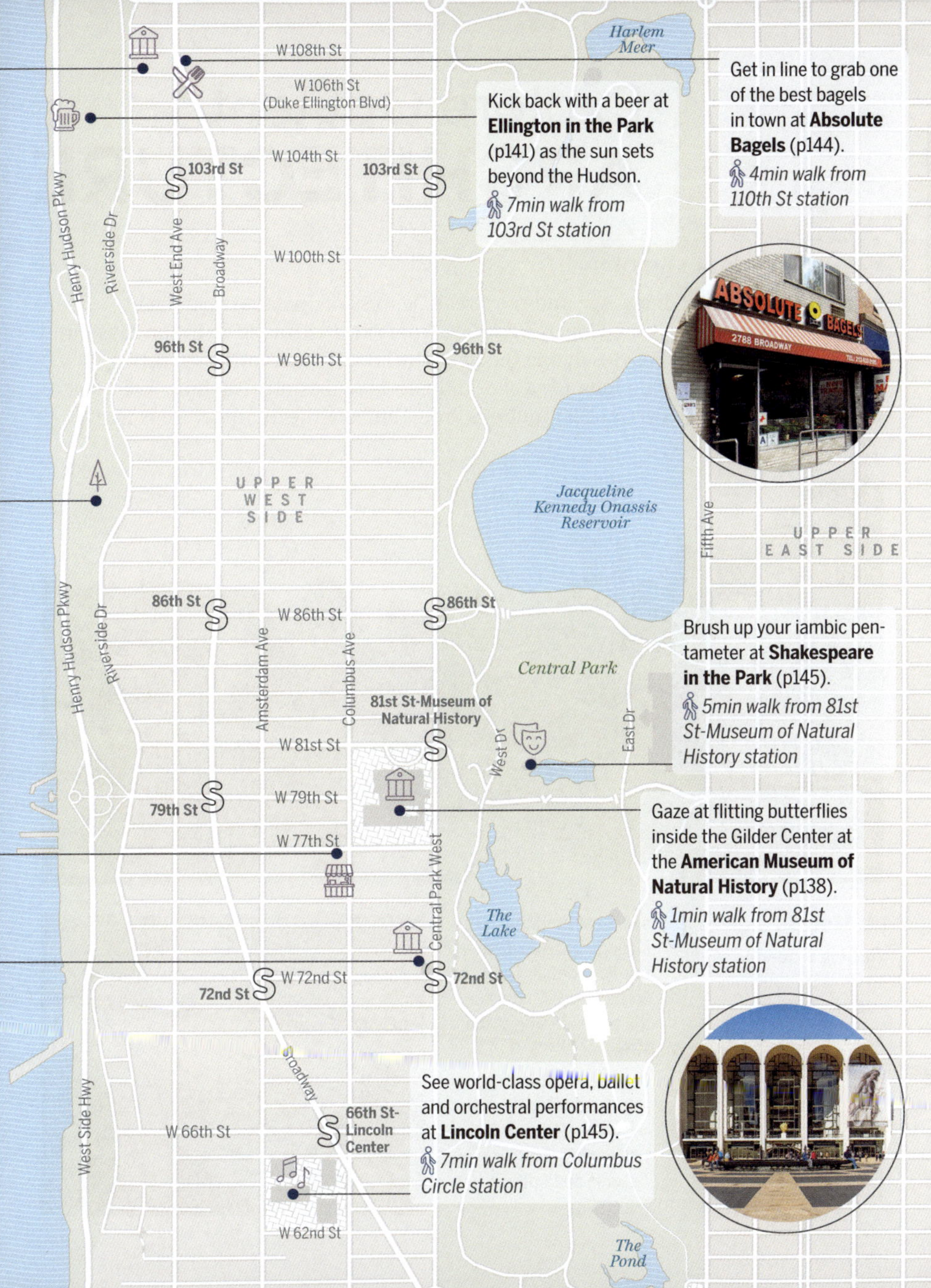

Kick back with a beer at **Ellington in the Park** (p141) as the sun sets beyond the Hudson.
7min walk from 103rd St station

Get in line to grab one of the best bagels in town at **Absolute Bagels** (p144).
4min walk from 110th St station

Brush up your iambic pentameter at **Shakespeare in the Park** (p145).
5min walk from 81st St-Museum of Natural History station

Gaze at flitting butterflies inside the Gilder Center at the **American Museum of Natural History** (p138).
1min walk from 81st St-Museum of Natural History station

See world-class opera, ballet and orchestral performances at **Lincoln Center** (p145).
7min walk from Columbus Circle station

27 Explore Opulent ARCHITECTURE

WALKABLE | REGAL | HISTORIC

Between the Gilded Age and the Great Depression, palatial apartment complexes transformed the Upper West Side from rural farmland to urban Elysium. Today their imposing facades define the neighborhood's boulevards, attracting affluent New Yorkers who long for a slice of historic real estate. Nabbing a piece of these coveted properties can cost millions, but admiring the architecture is free.

SUPAVADEE BUTRADEE/SHUTTERSTOCK ©

How to

Getting around 1/2/3 to 72nd St station and explore on foot.

When to go Visit on a bright morning or afternoon when each site is sunlit.

Look up Tourists are told to train their eyes on NYC's sidewalks, but to see these architectural stylings, gaze up. Admire top-floor details like cornices by standing on the opposite side of the street.

Cookie break Treat yourself to a decadent Levain cookie on 74th St while walking between the Ansonia and Apthorp.

JAMES ANDREWSI/SHUTTERSTOCK ©

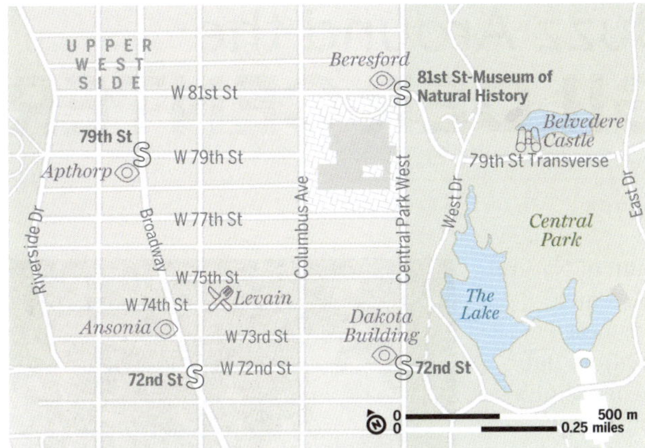

Apartment Hunting

Beaux arts beauty Start at the extravagantly ornamented **Ansonia** (1904). In the 1970s, Bette Midler belted it out to boys at the **Continental Baths**, a gay bath house and cabaret space that once occupied the basement.

Apartment envy Read screenwriter Nora Ephron's 2006 essay *Moving On, A Love Story* before peeking inside the wrought-iron gates of the **Apthorp** (1908), an Italian Renaissance Revival complex she called home for 24 years.

All in the timing Walk north for more Italian Renaissance splendor. Construction on Jewish immigrant and architect Emory Roth's **Beresford** finished a few weeks before the stock market crashed in 1929. Financial hardships ensued, and in 1940, a group of investors bought the building – along with the **San Remo**, another Roth design – for $25,000. Chump change.

Fairytale in the park Head to **Belvedere Castle** (1872), a Victorian folly in Central Park with panoramic viewing platforms. Look southwest to catch a glimpse of the **San Remo** (1931), its twin limestone towers poking above the tree line.

If walls could talk Exit the park at 72nd St to see the **Dakota Building** (1884), a co-op so exclusive even Cher was rejected by the board. Many famous residents have cycled through this Gothic-inspired building over the past century, though none are as closely tied to the fortress as John Lennon. He was tragically murdered outside the front gates in 1980.

Top left Belvedere Castle
Bottom left Levain cookie

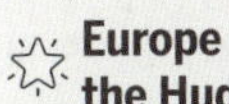

Europe on the Hudson

Growing up as a cellist studying at the Juilliard School and living on the Upper West Side, I was amazed by the grandeur of the prewar apartment buildings here. They looked like architecture I'd seen in Europe. I came to know them by their real names, each starting with a very serious The.

Check out the Ansonia's top cupola, where a skylight was blackened during WWII as part of NYC's precautions against air raids.

■ **Michelle Young**
Michelle Young is the founder of Untapped New York and a Professor of Architecture at Columbia University. She lives in Crown Heights, Brooklyn. @michelleyoungnewyork

28 Buzz Around the GILDER CENTER

IMMERSIVE | INSECTS | SCIENCE

The American Museum of Natural History (AMNH) – a science center spanning four city blocks – is best known for its dinosaur collection. But inside the Gilder Center, the museum's newest addition, it's all about the little stuff. Wander this 230,000-sq-ft architectural canyon, completed in 2023, for a fresh look at a classic museum.

XACKERY IRVING/SHUTTERSTOCK ©

How to

Getting here Take the B/C to 81st St-Museum of Natural History. If you only plan on visiting the Gilder Center, enter at 79th St and Columbus Ave.

When to go The museum is open from 10am to 5:30pm. Try visiting during the week to avoid crowds.

Bring the kids Interactive exhibits are a hit with elementary-school crews and anyone young at heart.

Extra Tickets The Butterfly Vivarium and *Invisible Worlds* both require separate entrance tickets. Pre-purchase online at amnh.org.

Beautiful Biology

Insect insight Leave the fly swatter at home: insects aren't pests inside the Gilder Center's 1st-floor **Insectarium** – they're the stars of the show. Watch 18 live insect species move about their day, including the world's largest display of leafcutter ants – a fleet-footed ensemble that carries their leaf clippings like they're marching in a parade. An 8000lb resin honey-bee hive is this section's most photogenic item. Walk around the giant artwork, outfitted with touch screens and serenaded by gentle buzzing, to learn about bee behavior.

Butterfly bonanza Beeline next for the **Davis Family Butterfly Vivarium**, a 2nd-floor exhibition where 80 live

Above Gilder Center **Top right** American Museum of Natural History **Bottom right** Davis Family Butterfly Vivarium

NURPHOTO/GETTY IMAGES ©

Style for Science

The AMNH's architecture is a lot like nature – a wacky collection of distinct parts that somehow, miraculously, work together. It started in the 1870s, originally designed by architects J Wrey Mould and Calvert Vaux (of Central Park fame), then new additions developed over the years, turning the museum into a stylistic Frankenstein. Spin around the complex to see a quilt of Gothic and Roman-esque decorations knitted to a futuristic glass cube and the Gilder Center. Sit in **Theodore Roosevelt Park** to take it in.

species of fragile-winged wonders float about the space, landing on outstretched arms. Don't leave without peeking at the pupae incubator – or nursery – where you might see a butterfly emerge triumphantly from its chrysalis. The room is kept at a balmy, humid 80°F – take off long sleeves before entering.

Universe on a screen More immersive experiences await at **Invisible Worlds**, a 3rd-floor exhibition that takes visitors on a 12-minute ride around a 23ft-oval screen. The 360-degree video travels through a Brazilian rainforest, follows migrating jellyfish and explores the synapses of a brain – among other destinations. A touch-sensitive floor is particularly magical.

ISMAIL FERDOUS/BLOOMBERG/ GETTY IMAGES ©

29 Riverside Park STROLL

GARDENS | DINING | SCULPTURES

This romantic esplanade hugging the Hudson River provides a soothing escape from Manhattan's endless bustle. Although overshadowed by nearby Central Park, Riverside Park shines bright thanks to waterfront views from triple-tiered paths, recreational facilities and classically inspired monuments. Take to this leafy green ribbon at sunset to enjoy nature's spectacular light show.

How to

Getting here Take the 1/2/3 to 72nd St station and walk west. The entire trail covers 2 miles.

When to go The park's amenities are most enjoyable between April and October.

Pick your path Green meadows link 59th St to 158th St, but for best sites, stick to upper promenades between 72nd and 105th Sts.

Pedal power The riverfront thoroughfare is a relaxed place for cycling. Rent a Citi Bike from stations along Riverside Dr.

Statues & Sunsets

Magnificent monuments Start your journey at 72nd St, where the park widens to include a waterfront bike path, grassy knolls and multi-tiered promenades. A bronze sculpture of **Eleanor Roosevelt** (1996) appears lost in thought. **Joan of Arc** (1915) gallops defiantly to the north.

Greek inspiration At 89th St, look toward Riverside Dr to see 12 Corinthian columns encircling the **Soldiers' & Sailors' Monument** (1902). The site, modeled after the Choragic monument of Lysicrates in Athens, honors Civil War Union Army members. It acts as a companion piece to **General Grant's Tomb**, the mausoleum of famed Civil War

Top right Soldiers' & Sailors' Monument **Bottom right** Riverside Park

FELIX LIPOV/SHUTTERSTOCK ©

Joan of Park

The Joan of Arc statue, which stands regally at 93rd St, offers many opportunities for celebration and reflection. First, there's Joan herself, patron saint of France. Dedicated in 1915, this was the first statue devoted to a non-fictional woman in New York City. Fittingly, it was created by a woman – award-winning American sculptor Anna Hyatt Huntington. The statue's granite pedestal, designed by John van Pelt, incorporates limestone blocks from the Rouen tower where Joan was imprisoned.

■ **Lucie Levine**
Lucie is a native New Yorker, historian and writer who founded the historical tour and event company Archive on Parade. @archiveonparade

general and 18th US president Ulysses, located at 122nd St.

Budding romance In spring and autumn, volunteers known as the Garden People tend to the **91st St Community Garden**. If visiting around April or May, blushing petals erupting from trees on **Cherry Walk** (100th to 125th Sts) will make your heart flutter.

Dinner with a view Finish your adventure at **Ellington in the Park** (11am-11pm Apr-Nov), a casual, neighborly outdoor restaurant overlooking the Hudson.

JAMES ANDREWS1 /SHUTTERSTOCK ©

DON'T LEAVE
New York Without

01 A taco from Los Tacos No 1
Line up for an authentic Mexican taco from the stand at Chelsea Market.

02 A black-and-white cookie
Be it a bakery, a bodega or an episode of *Seinfeld*, New York's black-and-white cookies are everywhere.

03 A 'We Are Happy to Serve You' Cup
The Anthora – a Grecian-style cardboard cup often found in delis – has served coffee to New Yorkers since the 1960s.

04 A New Yorker tote bag
This canvas tote is the ubiquitous purse for New York intellectuals and a status symbol for word nerds.

05 Magnolia's Banana Pudding
Sex and the City put Magnolia Bakery cupcakes on the map, but let's get real: it's all about the banana pudding.

06 A vintage tee from Beacon's Closet
Digging around these racks for dirt-cheap

designer labels is a rite-of-passage for frugal fashionistas.

07 Superiority Burger's vegan patty
Superiority Burger is White Castle for non-meat eaters. The vegan patty is so tasty you might as well order two.

08 A broken bodega umbrella
Owning a stash of cheap black umbrellas is a sign you've weathered New York like a local.

09 NYC Clothing
A Yankees cap. A Scarr's Pizza T-shirt. Nothing says 'I Love NY' like owning merch repping your favorite local institution.

10 Junior's cheesecake
Order a slice of the best NYC-style cheesecake at the original 1950 outpost of Juniors' in downtown Brooklyn.

11 A Broadway playbill
The Broadway show ends when the curtain comes down, but the iconic black-and-yellow program lasts forever.

Listings

BEST OF THE REST

Grab-and-Go Goodies

Absolute Bagels $

Bagels made by Thai immigrants might make connoisseurs uneasy, but one thing's certain: there's a line down the block because they are among the city's best.

Mama's TOO! $

You'll understand why people crowd outside this bite-sized pizza shop after tearing into the Angry Nonna (a square slab of hot honey-drizzled pepperoni). Make yourself happy – order two.

Pre-show Dinners

Tatiana $$$

Good luck getting a table at the Afro-Caribbean-inspired restaurant within Lincoln Center's David Geffen Hall, featured on nearly every 'best of' list in the city. Consolation prize? The adjacent lobby bar.

Cafe Luxembourg $$$

Upper-crust locals have been knocking back cocktails and nibbling steak tartare at this French bistro since the 1980s. Proximity to Lincoln Center makes it a perfect pre-opera destination.

Old John's Diner $$

1950s charm pours out of the Lincoln Center area's go-to luncheonette. Order the kids a classic egg cream and have yourself a Manhattan.

UWS Comfort Food

Barney Greengrass $$

This UWS institution from 1908 is best known as the undisputed 'Sturgeon King,' and the smoked whitefish that lives up to the title. Join regulars kvetching over breakfast and lunch.

Jacob's Pickles $$

Jacob elevates the humble pickle to exalted status at this loud, boisterous, good-time eatery. Expect briney cukes, heaping portions of comfort food and a solid craft beer selection.

Asian Fusion

Chick Chick $$

Korean- and Nashville-inspired chicken sandwiches rule this low-key poultry palace, while dishes like kimchi fried rice and ramen round out the cross-cultural menu.

Bánh $$

Travel to Hanoi on the Upper West Side's far reaches with Bánh's home-style Vietnamese food. Chow down the sticky mung bean rice cakes, bun cha or a toasted bánh mì.

Beloved Bakeries

Levain $

The original location of this national cookie chain remains its most charming. Each dough ball is a 6oz lesson in decadence, with the chocolate chip walnut earning highest marks.

Silver Moon Bakery $

Folks line up in droves for sweets by Judith Norell, who decided to hang up her harpsichord and flee to a Paris baking school before opening this tiny patisserie.

Cocktails & Craft Beer

Nobody Told Me $$

Be thankful you got the memo: this is the coolest cocktail joint within a 10-block radius.

Grab a front booth in warm weather – picture windows open to the street.

Gebhard's Beer Culture $

The UWS gets serious about suds thanks to Beer Culture's 16 taps of New York–heavy craft. Wash it all down with burgers, nachos and hot dogs.

Artisanal Coffee

Plowshares

Plowshares got into the specialty coffee game way back in 2008, when this cozy espresso spot opened in the Bloomingdale district of the UWS. There's a second location in Harlem.

Irving Farm New York

Tucked into a little ground-floor shop, the UWS location of this popular coffee mini-chain is bigger on the inside. Walk beyond the coffee-and-pastries counter to a light-filled backroom.

Flea & Food Markets

Grand Bazaar NYC

One of NYC's oldest open-air shopping spots, this well-stocked flea market is perfect for browsing away a lazy Sunday. You'll find a little bit of everything: furnishings, clothing, etc.

Zabar's

A bastion of gourmet kosher foodie-ism since Ukrainian Jewish immigrants opened its doors in 1934. Stop in for a heavenly array of cheeses, meats, olives, caviar, smoked fish and fresh-from-the-oven knishes.

Performing Arts

Lincoln Center

White travertine buildings dominate this modernist complex housing NYC's finest classical performances. Dress up for a night at the Metropolitan Opera, New York Philharmonic or New York City Ballet.

Gebhard's Beer Culture

Shakespeare in the Park

Every summer, Central Park's open-air Delacorte Theater hosts two high-quality productions of Shakespeare's plays. Admission is free, but prepare to wait in line or win the digital TodayTix lottery for same-day seats.

Quirky Museums

Nicholas Roerich Museum

Hidden on a residential street near Riverside Park, this three-story townhouse displays 150 paintings by Nicholas Konstantinovich Roerich (1874–1947), a Russian-born painter whose depiction of the Himalayas recalls Georgia O'Keeffe. Free.

American Folk Art Museum

Three small galleries with rotating exhibits celebrate artists without formal training. You might see kaleidoscopic quilts, hand-carved decoy ducks or centuries-old sketchbooks. Live Jazz every first and third Wednesday of the month. Free.

New-York Historical Society

NYC's oldest museum, founded in 1804, houses an extensive collection of art and artifacts examining culture and politics in New York and the US. Set aside an hour to explore.

30 Picnic in CENTRAL PARK

SNACKING | URBAN HIKING | WILDLIFE

Central Park's 843 acres of meadows, gardens, forests and lakes might be the antidote to concrete-jungle chaos, but finding tranquility is tricky if you stick to the well-worn paths below 72nd St. Seek out solitude while picnicking along the weeping-willow waterfront of the Pool – an uptown Arcadia more like the Adirondacks than the heart of Manhattan.

PANDORA PICTURES/SHUTTERSTOCK ©

How to

Getting here Take the B/C line to 103rd St station. From there, enter the park at 103rd or 100th Sts.

When to go Eat alfresco on sunny days between April and October. The trails near the Pool are pleasurable year-round.

When nature calls Find public restrooms on the Great Hill near 105th St.

Deep dive Download the Bloomberg Connects app for a free audio guide to Central Park.

GG5795/SHUTTERSTOCK ©

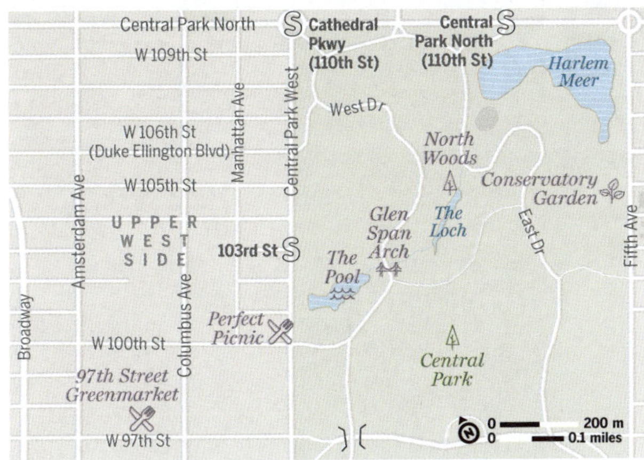

Pleasures in the Park

Find your food Peek inside **Perfect Picnic** on Central Park West to find park essentials like blankets, baskets and lunch grub. On Fridays, forage for locally grown produce, handmade cheese and artisanal bread at the **97th Street Greenmarket**.

Pick a spot Picnickers usually commune in the sun-drenched meadows around **the Pool**. If you require a seat, stick to the south side and claim the stand-alone wood bench framed by bald-cypress trees. Head toward Fifth Ave from the Pool for pretty petals inside the European-style **Conservatory Garden**.

Meet the neighbors Central Park's northwest corner is first-class real estate for wildlife. Mallard ducks preside over the Pool while grey squirrels and chipmunks reign among the woodlands. Turtles catch rays on rocky outcroppings when it's sunny and raccoons scamper around the treetops at twilight.

Take a hike Once you're satiated, follow the Pool's eastern path as it pours down a 20ft cascade and rushes underneath the rustic **Glen Span Arch**. This stream, known as **the Loch**, swerves through the **North Woods**, a 40-acre forest. Follow the meandering waterway north and you'll walk through a popular birding spot. Central Park, located along the Atlantic Flyway (an important route for migrating birds), acts as a resting pad for weary winged travelers. Twitchers can spot over 200 avian species resting among the leaves in spring and autumn. Further north, you'll pass a tiny waterfall and end up at the **Harlem Meer**, an idyllic lake near 110th St.

Far left Central Park
Left Glen Span Arch

Before the Park

In the 1850s, Central Park was covered with pig farms, a garbage dump, a bone-boiling operation and Seneca Village – the largest community of African American property owners in pre-Civil War New York. All that changed when construction began in 1858, after a public contest awarded landscape designer Frederick Law Olmstead and architect Calvert Vaux the honor of creating this oasis. Two difficult decades followed, forcibly displacing the area's roughly 1600 residents and employing 20,000 laborers to transform this terrain into a park. Today, Central Park has over 18,000 trees, 136 acres of woodland, 21 playgrounds and seven bodies of water – and over 40 million visitors annually.

HARLEM

ARTISTIC | FLAVORSOME | SOULFUL

HARLEM Trip Builder

TAKE YOUR PICK OF MUST-SEES AND HIDDEN GEMS

Harlem is a cradle for African American culture and a refuge for immigrants, a healing bowl of comfort food and a foreign land of opportunity. Some dignified mansions whisper of eras before high-rises replaced rolling hills, but they're often overpowered by a symphony of hip-hop, salsa and brass-band jazz. Stroll to the beat.

Neighborhood Notes

Best for Soul food, Latin American culture and arts.

Transportation A/C and B/D trains cover the west, the 2/3 runs along Lenox and the 6 runs through East Harlem.

Getting around Walk or take the m116 bus to travel east and west.

Tip Stroll Frederick Douglass Blvd from 110th to 120th Sts for restaurants and bars.

Order cocktails at Lucille's (p161) on Wednesday or Thursday evenings, when live jazz energizes the cafe.
11min walk from 14th St B/C station
See the memorial for poet Langston Hughes at the Schomburg Center for Research in Black Culture (p155).
1min walk from 135th St 2/3 station
See the ivories Duke Ellington once tickled in the tiny, pay-what-you-wish National Jazz Museum (p154).
6min walk from 125th St 2/3 station
Get an eyeful of brightly colored African textiles around Malcolm Shabazz Harlem Market (p156).
1min walk from 116 St 2/3 station
Dine on a plate of Puerto Rican fare before dancing to salsa at La Marqueta (p153).
4min walk from 116th St 6 station
Dive into delicious Peruvian food at Contento (p161), the most wheelchair-friendly restaurant in NYC.
5min walk from 110th St 6 station
W 135th St
E 135th St
135th St
W 134th St
W 133rd St
W 129th St
Harlem River
Schomburg Center
HARLEM
Adam Clayton Powell Jr Blvd (Seventh Ave)
Malcolm X Blvd (Lenox Ave)
Fifth Ave
Madison Ave
W 126th St
Martin Luther King Jr Blvd (W 125th St)
125th St
125th St
W 124th St
Marcus Garvey Park
W 122nd St
St Nicholas Ave
Third Ave
W 116th St
116th St
116th St
E 116th St (Luis Munoz Marin Blvd)
E 115th St
Lexington Ave
Park Ave
W 114th St
W 113th St
SPANISH HARLEM
E 112th St

31 Get a Taste of EL BARRIO

MARKETS | RESTAURANTS | CULTURE

East Harlem became Spanish Harlem – or El Barrio – after WWII, as waves of Puerto Ricans relocated to NYC. The neighborhood still crackles with San Juan-style *lechón* (suckling pig) and *pastelillos* (meat turnovers) aplenty, along with hearty helpings of Cuban, Mexican and other Latin American flavors. Dig in on a walking tour.

CITIZEN OF THE PLANET ALAMY STOCK PHOTO ©

Visit El Museo del Barrio

In 1969 a group of Puerto Rican activists opened **El Museo** (pictured) – the first Latin American cultural institution in the US. Today the museum anchors Spanish Harlem's southern edges between 104th and 105th Sts on Museum Mile. The permanent collection features over 8500 pieces, covering everything from Taíno artifacts to contemporary photography.

Trip Notes

Getting around Take the 6 to 110th St (near Amor Cubano) or 116th St (near La Marqueta). Plan on walking a mile between all destinations.

When to go Start around lunchtime. To hear salsa music at La Marqueta, visit on Saturday from noon to 6pm.

Language If you're a fluent Spanish speaker, this is the place to use it. *Español* is often the dominant language.

Money Bring cash – not all food stands take cards.

E 126th St
125th St
Martin Luther King Jr Blvd (E 125th St)
E 124th St
First Ave
05 Biting into the *rellenos de papa* (fried stuffed potatoes) or *morcilla* (blood sausage) at **Lechonera La Isla** is as good as a gastro tour in the Puerto Rican mountains.
LECHONERA La Isla
American & SPANISH Food
E 121st St
E 120th St
03 It's all about meat-stuffed fritters and fruit juices at Puerto Rican mainstay **Cuchifritos**, an El Barrio fixture since 1961.
E 119th St
HARLEM
Second Ave
E 118th St
Park Ave
04 Watch servers at **Taco Mix** carve thin slices of slow-roasted pork as they prep an order of Mexican-style *al pastor* (spit-roasted) tacos.
E 117th St
116th St
Luis Munoz Marin Blvd (E 116th St)
E 115th St
SPANISH HARLEM
Lexington Ave
Third Ave
02 Head underneath Park Ave's railroad tracks, where Caribbean comfort food and salsa music fill **La Marqueta** with Latinx pride.
01 Wash down seafood paella with a mojito at **Amor Cubano**, then come back for live Afro-Cuban tunes on weekend evenings.
Jefferson Park
E 112th St
E 111th St
110th St
E 110th St
FROM LEFT: EDEN/WIKIMEDIA/CC BY 2.0 ©, JASON LAM/FLICKR/BY-NC-SA 2.0 ©
0 200 m
0 0.1 miles
UPPER EAST SIDE

Feel the Pulse of Harlem's Renaissance

PEOPLE AND PLACES THAT SHAPED AN ARTISTIC REVOLUTION

Ever since the Harlem Renaissance jazzed up New York in the early 20th century, this neighborhood has been an incubator of African American culture, launching talents and trends with global appeal. This is where Billie Holiday crooned, Duke Ellington played and Langston Hughes penned blues-battered poetry. Vibrant and loud, brooding and melancholy – walk these streets and history sings.

Left National Jazz Museum **Centre** Apollo Theater **Right** Studio Museum

HERE NOW/SHUTTERSTOCK ©

Harlem's Revolution

The Harlem Renaissance was more than an artistic movement – it was a cultural explosion that started around 1918, blazed through the 1930s and echoes onward today. As African Americans shot north during the Great Migration – leaving behind the segregated Jim Crow South – Harlem became their Promised Land.

By the 1920s, the neighborhood was home to the largest concentration of African Americans in the US, and by 1930, they made up 70% of the population. Many passed through the YMCA on 135th St and Adam Clayton Powell Jr Blvd.

This building – where literary bigwigs Claude McKay (*Home to Harlem;* 1928) and Ralph Ellison (*The Invisible Man;* 1952) could cross paths with actors like Paul Robeson and Eartha Kitt – is a microcosm of what happened in the broader neighborhood. Black intellectuals and artists of all stripes came together, helping each other find something with pens, paintbrushes and pianos long denied by American oppression: freedom.

Sounds of the Jazz Age

Jazz music became Harlem's heartbeat, its syncopated rhythms fusing African and European music in a protest against marching band conformity – and Duke Ellington became its star performer. Head to the tiny **National Jazz Museum** – a one-room, Smithsonian-affiliated love letter to improvisational players to see Ellington's cream-white baby grand piano – and imagine him composing *Harlem* (1950). His 14-minute symphonic suite celebrates the place he called home, and where legends like Ella Fitzgerald and Louis Armstrong played at the **Apollo Theater**, amplifying voices from the African diaspora since 1934.

JAMES KIRKIKIS/SHUTTERSTOCK ©

BEYOND MY KEN/WIKIMEDIA/CC BY-SA 4.0 ©

Seeing Harlem's Beauty

As spontaneous trumpet solos changed NYC's sonic landscape, visual artists redecorated the neighborhood in their image. Aaron Douglas married African heritage with art deco stylings in murals like *Evolution of Negro Dance* (1935), sprawling across a room at the Harlem YMCA. Sculptor Augusta Savage created busts praising African American faces, with interpretations of luminaries like WEB DuBois putting her a head above the rest. Today the **Studio Museum** (opened in 1968) champions art by Renaissance visionaries – including a sizable collection by James Van Der Zee, who glamorized the African American community in photographs, imbuing each portrait of Harlem with pride.

> Jazz music became Harlem's heartbeat, its syncopated rhythms fusing African and European music in a protest against marching band conformity

Powerful Pens

Writers ultimately became the record keepers of Harlem's Jazz Age jamboree – defining the joys and struggles of African Americans through poetry and prose. Most influential was Alain Locke, 'dean' of the Renaissance, whose 1925 anthology *The New Negro* tied together essays, fiction and poems by African American authors, inciting a major literary movement. The writers he included went on to become some of Harlem's most revered: Zora Neal Hurston, Countee Cullen and Langston Hughes – 'poet laureate' of the Harlem Renaissance. Hughes spent his last 20 years on the top floor of a rowhouse at 20 E 127th St, where he penned *Harlem* – an 11-line poem about the dangers of a 'dream deferred.'

Artistry Archived

For a deeper exploration of historic Black Harlem and the creators who built its foundation, visit the **Schomburg Center for Research in Black Culture** (*nypl.org/locations/schomburg*), a branch of the New York Public Library near the Harlem YMCA. The extensive collection of books, manuscripts, sounds and images covers all the Harlem Renaissance greats – Langston Hughes' ashes are even interred under the floor in a book-shaped box. Rotating exhibitions highlight materials from the collection; conversations about trailblazers take place digitally and in an on-site theater. Tours of the space suspended in 2020, but they're expected to return sometime in the fall of 2024.

32 Find the Beat in LE PETIT SENEGAL

FOOD | MUSIC | MARKETS

Skip around south-central Harlem and you'll hear a musical melange of foreign languages. English, French and Wolof (spoken in West Africa) all join forces in a microneighborhood known as Le Petit Senegal, or Little Senegal. Francophone immigrants from Africa began building a community here around the 1980s. Join them around restaurants, shops and performance spaces with African flair.

How to

Getting around Take the B/C to 116th St or the A/D to 125th St for Des Ambassades.

When to go Choose a sunny weekend between spring and autumn.

Foodie favorites It's easy to fall in love with Senegalese food, but it's hard finding ingredients to make it at home – unless you head to **Adja Khady**, a wholesale African market selling the syrups, spices and coffees used in dishes and drinks at neighborhood restaurants.

Markets, Meats & Music

By day Pick up something sweet from **Des Ambassades**, a Senegalese restaurant and French African bakery serving buttery croissants and fruit tarts, then start walking east. You'll eventually reach **Malcolm Shabazz Harlem Market**, a canopied bazaar packed with colorful African goods. Trawl the stalls for textiles, jewelry, oils, sculptures and musical instruments. After scoping the treasures, walk north to **Marcus Garvey Park**, named after the African American nationalist who advocated for the 'back to Africa' movement, encouraging African Americans to return to their ancestral lands. On

Top right Marcus Garvey Park
Bottom right Malcolm Shabazz Harlem Market

HERE NOW/SHUTTERSTOCK ©

HEMIS / ALAMY STOCK PHOTO ©

Africa in the Spotlight

Enjoy Pan-African creativity year-round at events hosted by the **Caribbean Cultural Center African Diaspora Institute**, an arts and education center in Harlem. Particularly joyful is the annual **Afribembé Festival**. This day-long August block party celebrates an intergenerational mix of Black dancers, musicians and artisans. Check the schedule for art openings, workshops and guest performances. cccadi.org/events

sunny Sunday afternoons, the sounds of a drum circle pulse through the air. These free-to-join **jam sessions** mix West African and Caribbean traditions. Finally, on Saturday or Sunday, head southeast to **Teranga**, a casual cafeteria that packs grain bowls with West African favorites. Take yours to go: the restaurant is steps from Central Park's postcard-pretty **Harlem Meer**.

By night Make a reservation at **Africa Kine**, a Senegalese spot open since the 1990s. The restaurant's location has changed a few times since then, but the cooking remains the same – expect meat so tender it falls right off the bone. Cap off the evening by grooving next door at **Shrine**; this live music venue hosts everything from calypso to Latin jazz.

33 A Tale of TWO MANSIONS

ARCHITECTURE | HISTORY | RIVALRY

The Morris-Jumel Mansion (former home of Aaron Burr) and Hamilton Grange (former home of Founding Father Alexander Hamilton) might be a mile apart, but the stories of their inhabitants are inextricably tied together. On 11 July 1804, Burr shot Hamilton in a deadly duel. Burr won the battle, but who won the real estate war? Visit both and decide for yourself.

How to

Getting here Take the C to 163rd St-Amsterdam Ave for the Morris-Jumel Mansion, then take the C south to 145th St for the Hamilton Grange National Memorial.

When to go Make this an afternoon: start at Morris-Jumel around opening (1pm Tue-Thu, 11am Fri-Sun), then try to catch a tour at Hamilton Grange (1:30pm or 3:30pm Wed-Fri, plus an additional 2:30pm on weekends).

See the show End your day at the Richard Rodgers Theater to see *Hamilton,* Lin-Manuel Miranda's hip-hop musical about the Burr-Hamilton rivalry.

Burr vs Hamilton

Burr's short stint The **Morris-Jumel Mansion** (morrisjumel.org) is Manhattan's oldest surviving house, built on a bluff in 1765 for British colonel Roger Morris. George Washington turned the site into his headquarters during the American Revolution, before it was bought by Stephen and Eliza Jumel 1810. After Stephen's death, Eliza remarried Burr in the mansion's parlor (1833) – but the former US Vice President barely enjoyed the abode. Eliza dumped him four months later. One of her divorce attorneys? Alexander Hamilton's same-named son.

Top right Hamilton Grange
Bottom right Morris-Jumel Mansion

HERE NOW/SHUTTERSTOCK ©

MARIUSZ LOPUSIEWICZ/SHUTTERSTOCK ©

Founding Frenemies

Burr and Hamilton are America's original political nemeses, rivals since their days as NYC law colleagues in the 1780s. Historians say the feud likely began when Burr defeated Hamilton's father-in-law, Philip Schuyler, for New York State Senator in 1791. Over the next decade, Hamilton vigorously opposed Burr's political ambitions. In 1804, a letter published in the *Albany Register* quoted Hamilton calling Burr 'a dangerous man, and not to be trusted.' Haughty Burr didn't take it well. Headstrong Hamilton didn't apologize. The rest is history.

Tours take place at noon Tuesday to Sunday ($10). Fun fact: Lin-Manuel Miranda wrote Hamilton songs *The Room Where It Happens* and *Wait For It* in Burr's former bedroom.

Hamilton's last home

Hamilton Grange (nps.gov/hagr), a stately Federal-style home, sat on 32 acres 9 miles from NYC. Not that the acreage would matter much to Hamilton in the long run – he only enjoyed the land for two years before succumbing to his fatal wound. The edifice moved twice after Hamilton's death, landing at its current location in 2008. Visitors can join guided tours of the 1st floor. Admission is free.

Listings

BEST OF THE REST

Best Breakfasts

Amy Ruth's Restaurant $

Crispy fried chicken on syrup-smothered waffles: that's the main reason to come to this Alabama-style, no-fuss brunch spot, churning out almost all the greasy grub Harlem can handle since 1998.

Harlem Biscuit Company $$

Buttery biscuits are all the rage for locals near St Nicholas Park. If you order one with the Cajun- and Southern-inspired fixings, plan to unbuckle your belt.

Lido $$

Weekend brunch means serious business at this Italian-style spot, anchoring a long stretch of noteworthy restaurants on Adam Clayton Powell Jr Blvd since 2011. Order the bottomless mimosas ($25).

Bo's Bagels $

When native New Yorker Andrew Martinez couldn't find a proper bagel shop, he started making his own. He perfected the art and now runs Harlem's go-to for rolls with holes.

Southern-style Cooking

Melba's $$

Fried chicken drowning in gravy, crispy catfish (maybe on a waffle), sides of collard greens, mac-and-cheese – and plenty of syrup for you to drown in, too. Soul food perfection.

Sylvia's $$

Founded by Sylvia Woods in 1962, this Harlem icon has attracted scores of locals, celebrities and even a few presidents with its down-home Southern cooking.

Ginny's Supper Club $$

See what all the noise is about upstairs at **Red Rooster**, famous for elevated African American staples, or dip into this basement speakeasy, delivering similar plates plus Jazz Age glamor.

Harlem Shake $

The all-American burger gets a glow up: no matter which concoction you choose, there will be two cheese-hugging patties sandwiched by a lightly toasted potato bun. Down it with a milkshake.

Plant-Based Plates

Slutty Vegan $$

Ready to lose your vegan virginity? Head to the Harlem counter of this indulgent Atlanta-born, plant-based burger chain. Yes, you'll be called a 'slut.' No, they don't really mean it. Maybe.

VeganHood $$

Soul food is for everyone at this vegan comfort corner, where the 'fried chicken' is pea-protein based and the pudding is so rich you'd never guess there wasn't dairy.

Classy Dining

Clay $$$

Bi-level yet intimate New American restaurant plating some of the most refined local, seasonal cuisine north of 110th St. Nothing here is an afterthought – you can make a meal of the sides.

Vinatería $$

A splash of Spain, a dash of Italy and a high-end atmosphere make this a romantic evening spot, but you're coming for small plates and wine around Happy Hour (4pm-7pm Sun-Fri).

Contento $$$

The Peruvian dishes all stand out so the guests don't have to. Accessibility is at the forefront of this restaurant's design, making this NYC's most wheelchair-inclusive spot for elevated eating.

Beer, Cocktails & Coffee

Lucille's $$

Coffee by day, cocktails by night and relaxed vibes around the clock. Come at 8pm Wednesdays and Thursdays, when live jazz lifts the crowd from workday digerati to sexy sophisticates.

Sugar Monk $$

Get cozy in this low-lit space and choose from over 20 craft cocktails, plus house-made *amari* (after-dinner digestifs), liqueurs and bitters. Come for live jazz on Monday nights ($10 cover).

Harlem Hops $

Hard-to-find, small-batch breweries get their due at this beer hall with over a dozen unique suds on draft. There's bar food, too, but you should fill up elsewhere.

Double Dutch $

Down espressos with the work-from-coffee-shop crew in this slender cafe during the day. Sip espresso martinis next door at **Mess Hall** once night descends.

Vintage Threads & Hats

Trintage

'Trendy' and 'vintage' make the perfect portmanteau for this Harlem closet of women's clothes, where you'll find a colorful selection of stylish, reasonably priced threads.

Flamekeepers Hat Club

Owner Marc Williamson brings back Harlem Renaissance aesthetics with his collection of sophisticated hats, caps, bags and pocket squares suited for all occasions – especially when an actual suit is involved.

Harlem Haberdashery

Clothes, accessories and even alkaline water – you'll find it all at this on-trend boutique, whose owners regularly style big-name celebs for red carpet events.

Gothic Architecture & Green Spaces

Cathedral Church of St John the Divine

Step inside this Gothic cathedral to see the stained-glass Great Rose Window, with over 10,000 glass pieces covering its 40ft diameter, and enjoy rotating art exhibits under a soaring ceiling.

Met Cloisters

This Met-affiliated museum showcases medieval art and architecture inside a monastery-style building that evokes old-world Europe from its perch in Fort Tryon Park. Views of the Hudson River dazzle below. Same-day entry included with Met tickets.

Inwood Hill Park

Manhattan's last natural forest and salt marsh covers 196 acres on the northern reaches of the island, with trails that link to leafy Fort Tryon – lovely to hike as spring flowers begin blooming.

QUEENS
MULTICULTURAL | CULINARY | CREATIVE
43 St
SUNNYSIDE

citi
THE TOP-RANKED CANCER CARE CENTER IN THE NORTHEAST.
30 YEARS IN A ROW.
RENT NOW

QUEENS
Trip Builder

TAKE YOUR PICK OF MUST-SEES AND HIDDEN GEMS

NYC's largest borough proves it really is a small world after all. You'll find a bit of China in Flushing, Greece in Astoria and a dash of nearly every nation in Jackson Heights. Take a global food tour sans passport, then join the artsy set, gathered in museums and convening in clubs.

Neighborhood Notes

Best for International food and engaging art.

Transportation The N/R/W serves Astoria; the 7 serves Jackson Heights and Flushing; the M and L serve Ridgewood.

Plan ahead Queens is huge, and many destinations are far from Manhattan. Pick a neighborhood and plan on doing a half-day deep dive.

Appreciate massive stone sculptures and delicate paper lamps at the minimalist **Noguchi Museum** (p169).
1min walk from Socrates Sculpture Park

Visit the **Knockdown Center** (p173), a factory transformed into one of NYC's premier pop-up party destinations.
20min walk from Jefferson St L station

STEINWAY
Bowery Bay
Flushing Bay
Taste the culinary traditions of Asia at dozens of food stands within Flushing's **New World Mall** (p172).
1min walk from Flushing-Main St station
Bring a group to Greek restaurant **Taverna Kyclades** (p172) and order a bunch of family-style plates.
5min walk from Astoria-Ditmars Blvd station
Grand Central Pkwy
23rd Ave
Astoria Blvd
Whitestone Expwy
WOODSIDE
JACKSON HEIGHTS
Main St
Fall in love with Jim Henson's world of puppets at the **Museum of the Moving Image** (p169).
6min walk from Steinway St R station
Northern Blvd
114th St
Roosevelt Ave
Van Wyck Expwy
Munch on authentic Mexican tacos from **Birria-Landia** (p167), the original outpost of this corn-tortilla king.
4min walk from 74th St-Broadway 7 station
Roosevelt Ave
Broadway
Booth Memorial Ave
108th St
Grand Central Pkwy
FLUSHING
Meadow Lake
Junction Blvd
Long Island Expwy
ELMHURST
Let your nose lead you around the artisanal food stands populating Saturday's seasonal **Queens Night Market** (p173).
11min walk from 111th St station
MASPETH
Grand Ave
Queens Blvd
Long Island Expwy
Eliot Ave
Woodhaven Blvd
FOREST HILLS
Flushing Ave
Fresh Pond Rd
69th St
QUEENS
71st Ave
Metropolitan Ave
RIDGEWOOD
welcome to the Queens Night Market
Spend a weekend afternoon dancing to house music at Mister Sunday, a seasonal **Nowadays** (p170) party.
8min walk from Halsey St L station
Myrtle Ave
Forest Park
GLENDALE
0 2 km
0 1 mile

34 Have a Global Feast in JACKSON HEIGHTS

INTERNATIONAL | FLAVORFUL | FILLING

Over 160,000 people call Jackson Heights home. In this cacophonous neighborhood where the 7 train screeches overhead, street vendors hawk food fare and cheap wares, and you might hear upwards of 160 unique languages spoken (if not shouted) above the din. It's NYC's most diverse neighborhood, best explored by belly.

RICHARD LEVINE/ALAMY STOCK PHOTO RICHARD LEVINE/ALAMY STOCK PHOTO ©

Trip Notes

Getting here Take the 7 to 74th St-Broadway or the F to Jackson Heights-Roosevelt Ave. Plan on walking 1 mile between destinations.

When to go Start this food tour around late afternoon. Hours vary by business, but the timeframe when most places are open concurrently is 5pm to 6pm. Check business hours before stopping by.

Top tip Bring cash. Some of the small food carts selling culturally authentic cuisine (kababs, empanadas, pupusas – you name it) don't take cards.

Community Roots

Jackson Heights wasn't intended as a global sanctuary. The Queens Corporation, a real estate developer, designed the neighborhood in the early 20th century as a segregated community for upper- and middle-class white families. Jews and LGBTIQ+ crowds eventually moved in, followed by immigrants from South America, and Asia and India. Acceptance became de rigueur.

01 Stop by Bangladeshi food cart **Tong** for *fuchka*, a deep-fried mini puff filled with a sweet or savory stew (your choice).

02 Eye the case of colorful desserts such as *gulab jamun* (fried dough balls in syrup) at Pakistani cafe **Al-Naimat Sweets & Restaurant** while savoring curries or tandooris.

03 Head to **Birria-Landia** and order the beef-stuffed, Tijuana-style *birria* taco. Dip it in your cup of *consomé* (a broth) for a punch of flavor.

04 Bite into heart-shaped *onigri* (stuffed rice balls) or *onigirazu* (a rice-layered, nori-wrapped sandwich) at Japanese cafe **969 NYC Coffee**.

05 Wash down the day with a Mexican *michelada* mug (a beer-and-tomato juice cocktail) at aptly named **Michelada House II**.

35 Go on an Astoria ART CRAWL

MOVIES | SCULPTURES | MURALS

Directly across the East River from Manhattan's Upper East Side, Astoria is quintessential Queens: multicultural and bursting with creativity. You won't find Brooklyn-style brownstone grandeur here, only mid-rise brick and vinyl-sided buildings. But the neighborhood doesn't lean into the drabness – it beautifies each block with art. Spend a day admiring Astoria's innovation.

NAME/CREDIT ©

How to

Getting here Take the R to Steinway St or the N to 36 Ave for the Museum of the Moving Image (MoMI). Walking between destinations covers roughly 2 miles.

When to go Tackle this tour on Saturday or Sunday, when MoMI opens at noon. Budget half a day to explore the neighborhood.

Food and drink After exploring MoMI, grab a pita at **King Souvlaki**, a Greek-style food truck. For coffee, head to dog cafe **Château Le Woof** near Socrates Sculpture Park.

RUDY SULGAN/GETTY IMAGES ©

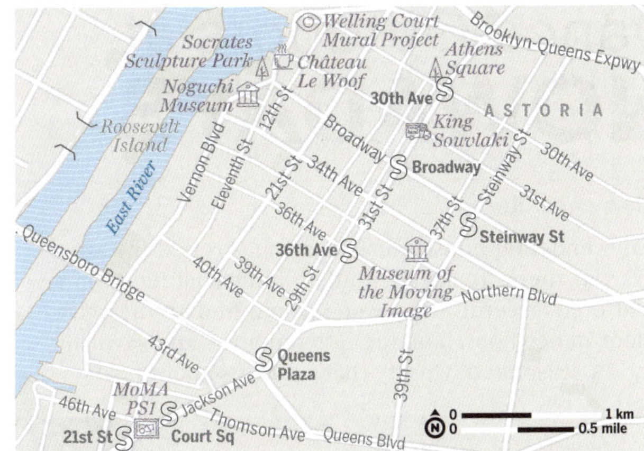

Wander Between Wonders

Behind the silver screen Start at the **Museum of the Moving Image**, dedicated to all things film, TV and video. It's easy to lose yourself in exhibits covering everything from director retrospectives to DIY sound mixing. If you're short on time, run to the gallery dedicated to *Muppets* creator Jim Henson.

Greek greenery Next up is tiny **Athens Square**. Astoria is best known as a Greek neighborhood, and this park pays homage with a bust of Aristotle, a seated sculpture of Socrates and an amphitheater where musicians play Greek tunes in summer.

Colorful streets Head east on 30th Ave to reach the **Welling Court Mural Project**, a collection of murals splayed across several streets like spokes on a wheel. The artsy assemblage includes spray paint royalty like NYC local Buff Monster.

Art park Amble over to **Socrates Sculpture Park**, packed with gigantic art installations overlooking the East River. In 1986, sculptor Mark di Suvero led a team of artists who salvaged this waterfront from its use as an illegal dumpsite. It's come a long way: on summer weekends, there's **free kayaking** in nearby Hallet's Cove. licboathouse.org

Meditation on minimalism End at the **Noguchi Museum**, a factory-turned-zen studio by minimalist designer Isamu Noguchi, who converted the once-neglected space. After his death in 1988, the site became a museum peppered with his sculptures and iconic paper lamps.

Top left Athens Square
Bottom left Museum of the Moving Image

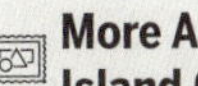

More Art in Long Island City

The freshest, funkiest museum in Queens is undoubtedly **MoMA PS1** – MoMA's punk rock little sibling. PS1 first hit the scene in 1976, when Alanna Heiss, a champion of art in alternative spaces, took possession of an abandoned Renaissance Revival school building in Long Island City. She then invited artists like Richard Serra and James Turrell to create site-specific works. The result was PS1's inaugural exhibition, *Rooms*. A few remnants of that first show remain, including Turrell's heavenly *Meeting*, which frames the naked sky through a hole in the 3rd floor's ceiling. Today PS1 continues playing host to experimental exhibitions, live performances and concerts.

36 Dance Outdoors at NOWADAYS

ELECTRONIC MUSIC | DANCING | RELAXING

If you didn't hear transcendental house music floating through the air, you'd never know Nowadays was there. Tucked behind an industrial fence on an otherwise quiet, graffiti-splattered street in Ridgewood, you'll find an inclusive crowd grooving on an outdoor dance floor, hanging in hammocks and savoring BBQ. This is Mister Sunday – a seasonal day party that's serious about beats.

ROBERT K CHIN - STOREFRONTS/ALAMY STOCK PHOTO ©

How to

Getting here Take the L to Halsey St.

When to go Mister Sunday runs 3pm to 11pm every Sunday from May to October. The event is outdoors, so sunny days are best. Arrive earlier for smaller crowds; things get busiest between 5pm and 6:30pm. If you didn't purchase tickets in advance, line up early to ensure you'll get in.

Tickets Head to nowadays.nyc for event updates and links to tickets, purchased via the Resident Advisor app.

SNOWFIRE/WIKIMEDIA/CC BY 4.0 © ©

The space Nowadays is a relaxed indoor-outdoor playground for adults on the Bushwick–Ridgewood border and an energetic spillover from artsy Brooklyn. Mister Sunday takes over its 16,000-sq-ft, dirt-and-gravel garden – complete with bar (cocktails and craft beer), food truck (Mexican bites), picnic tables and hammocks (killer, if you can snag one). The center of the action is a slightly bouncy dance floor, framed by a crystal-clear sound system and topped by a disco ball. There's also an attached 5000-sq-ft warehouse – primarily used for evening programming – with drinks, food and a hazy dance floor featuring another audiophile-approved sound system.

The vibe Most NYC parties come and go, but this shindig has been going strong since 2008 thanks to a strict door policy: there's zero tolerance for discrimination, consent is mandatory to touch fellow guests and there are no phones on the dance floor. The result? An all-are-welcome mix of music heads who dance like nobody's watching. Expect a sizable queer contingency, rave kids, dance-floor divas from the 1990s and the occasional fratty misfits. There might even be young parents, fresh from an ayahuasca journey, their too-cool-for-school child in tow.

The music Eamon Harkin and Justin Carter, Mister Sunday's co-founders and occasional DJs, started this day hang as a house-forward, disco-adjacent joy fest. The music remains similar: expect electronic eclecticism.

Top left Topos Bookstore **Bottom left** Vander Ende-Onderdonk House

A Day Around Ridgewood

It takes 30 to 45 minutes to reach Ridgewood from Midtown Manhattan. If you're traveling from afar, turn this journey into a day-long adventure. Start at the **Vander Ende-Onderdonk House**, NYC's oldest Dutch Colonial stone home, sitting on the neighborhood's western corner since 1709. Tours of the building take place at noon to 5pm Saturday and Sunday. If you're in the mood for brunch, try **Rolo's** – a sunny wood-fired restaurant serving eggs, burgers and crispy French toast on weekends from 11am to 3pm. Need coffee? Stop by **Topos Bookstore** to caffeinate while flipping through zines. Prefer beer? There's **Evil Twin Brewing**, a sunny spot for local hops.

Listings

BEST OF THE REST

Flushing's Best Eats

White Bear $

Flushing is one of NYC's main hubs for Chinese immigrants, evident in the delectable dumplings you'll find at this no-frills, cash-only food counter. Try the pork and veggie wontons.

New York Food Court $

Taiwan-style steak, Hunan fish noodles, Shanghainese lamb dumplings and more Asian delights bubble, crackle and simmer around a dozen food counters serving seriously spicy delicacies.

New World Mall Food Court $

Chinese, Japanese, Korean, Malaysian, Thai and Vietnamese – spin around the 30-odd food stalls in the basement of this three-floor mall and you'll find it all.

Eight Jane $

Stop by this take-out window for *jianbing* (an eggy, crepe-style, grab-and-go breakfast food folded with scallions, savory sauce and crunchy deep-fried crackers). Cash only.

Casa Enrique $$$

Order anything with the decadent, semi-sweet mole sauce, perhaps poured over chicken enchiladas, at this upscale Mexican restaurant. For something extra sweet, end with the spongy tres leches cake.

Adda Indian Canteen $$

Can't get into Michelin-starred Semma? Try this cheaper spot by the same owners, serving Indian dishes like *biryani* (goat with saffron-spiced rice) and vegan chutneys.

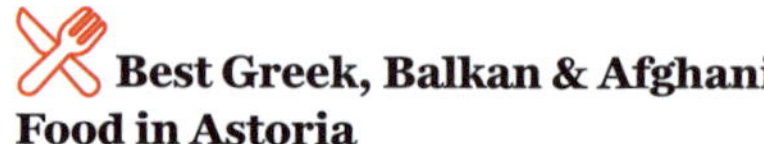

Best Greek, Balkan & Afghani Food in Astoria

Taverna Kyclades $$

You can get a taste of Athens in Astoria at over a dozen delicious Greek restaurants, but if you only choose one, this should be it. Everything comes family-style; don't skimp on the seafood.

Astoria Seafood $$

Greek-style wholesale fish supplier and eat-in market. Grab a bag, pick whatever raw seafood you'd like, then tell the cashier how you want it prepared (grilled, deep-fried, roasted, etc). BYOB.

Little Flower Cafe $

An Afghani spin on a New York City coffee shop: there's a Boston cream-style donut, stuffed instead with cardamom-and-rosewater custard, and a BEC with halal lamb bacon, egg and cheese.

Franky's Souvlaki $

Let your nose guide you to the royal blue food truck on Steinway St, where the smoke of skewered meats and veggies lures hungry customers to the Astoria outpost of this rolling gyro empire.

Cevabdzinica Sarajevo $

Fill your belly with hearty Balkan bites, like *cevapi* (a thin beef-and-lamb sausage resembling an American frank) along with cheese, meat or spinach *bureks* (stuffed pastries) at 'Sarajevo Grill.'

Ridgewood's Cannoli, Cocktails & Craft Brews

Rudy's Pastry Shop $

It started as a neighborly German bakery in 1934, and though the owners are now Italian (try a cannoli), it remains a beloved local fixture. Stop by for a cheesy croissant sandwich.

Aftermath $$

Liquor bottles and vinyls take pride of place behind mixologists, whipping up magic in a drinking den that's equally dedicated to great music and craft cocktails.

Bridge & Tunnel Brewery $

Sampling some of the 16 beers on tap at this tiny operation feels like downing brewskies in your best friend's basement. It's thrifty and grungy, intimate and welcoming; almost a second home.

Night on the Town

Queens Night Market $

Travel the world one food stand at a time at this Saturday night bazaar, with up to 100 vendors selling food and art alongside performances showcasing the borough's cultural wealth. April to October

Knockdown Center $$

This 50,000-sq-ft factory in industrial Maspeth hosts some of the hottest parties in town, including Horse Meat Disco (sweaty gay rave) and Basement (DJ-focused, strict door policy). Visit knockdown.center for events.

The Bonnie $$

Sidle up to the bar for specialty cocktails or grab a table for the full gastropub experience. Whether you're here for a $25 bottomless brunch or an all-night banger, Astoria's Bonnie provides.

Bohemian Hall & Beer Garden $$

Shlosh steins foaming with Czech pilsners at this great-for-groups beer garden – NYC's oldest, established in 1910. Come on a sunny summer afternoon, when all of Astoria crams together at picnic tables.

Museums with World's Fair Flavor

Queens Museum

Originally constructed for the 1939 World's Fair in Flushing Meadows-Corona Park, most people come here to see *Panorama of the City of New York* – a 9335-sq-ft model of NYC from 1964.

New York Hall of Science

Hundreds of hands-on exhibits housed in a structure from the 1964 World's Fair invite visitors to learn about engineering, marine biology, climate change, sports and more – particularly engaging for little ones.

Historic Parks & Inclusive Beaches

Fort Totten

Explore a preserved Civil War fortress on a history tour, canoe around the Long Island Sound, sun in meadows or spy birds near the waterfront.

Jacob Riis Park

Monied LGBTIQ+ New Yorkers head to Fire Island for summer, but the hordes that stay in town flock to this come-as-you-are 'People's Beach' – a queer haven on sunny weekends.

BROOKLYN
HIP | INNOVATIVE | DIVERSE
ONE WAY
ONE WAY
ICE CREAM
ICE CREAM

BROOKLYN
Trip Builder

TAKE YOUR PICK OF MUST-SEES AND HIDDEN GEMS

Brooklyn might be synonymous with artsy-fartsy hipsterdom, but NYC's most populous borough is more than beards and bikes. It's industrial chic and immigrant heritage, splattered in street art and colonized by the cutting edge. Hit up a warehouse party or saunter along East River shores, uncovering why Kings County is the global epicenter of 'cool.'

Neighborhood Notes

Best for Nightlife, art and picturesque neighborhoods.

Transportation L and J/M/Z serve North Brooklyn; 2/3, 4/5, A/C, B/D/F and N/Q/R serve South Brooklyn. The G runs north–south.

Getting around Walk, bike or train.

Tip Don't try seeing everything in a day: pick south (Dumbo, Brooklyn Heights) or north (Williamsburg, Bushwick).

Wax poetic like Walt Whitman about the views from **Brooklyn Bridge Park** (p178).
7min walk from High St station

Take in the view from **Brooklyn Heights Promenade** (p182), connected to NYC's original suburb.
11min walk from Borough Hall station

Skip through the sylvan landscape of **Prospect Park** (p187), designed by Central Park's creators.
5min walk from Grand Army Plaza station

Get your foodie fill at the open-air Smorgasburg (p191) bazaar.
8min walk from Bedford Ave station
Feast on coal-fired skewers at Laser Wolf (p190) while savoring Manhattan's distant skyline.
9min walk from Bedford Ave station
Slurp oysters and sip absinthe at 19th-century New Orleans–style Maison Premiere (p190).
10min walk from Bedford Ave station
Eye the quirky assemblage of NYC oddities, collected over decades, at tiny City Reliquary (p191).
8min walk from Lorimer St station
Dance till you drop at House of Yes (p188), Bushwick's inclusive party palace.
12min walk from Morgan Ave station
Snap a pic in front of the OY/YO sculpture outside Brooklyn Museum (p186) before exploring indoor exhibits.
1min walk from Eastern Parkway-Brooklyn Museum station
East River
GREENPOINT
N 10th St
Kent Ave
Bedford Ave
Graham Ave
WILLIAMSBURG
EAST WILLIAMSBURG
Grand St
Williamsburg Bridge
Grand St
SOUTH WILLIAMSBURG
Broadway
Flushing Ave
Jefferson St
Flushing Ave
BUSHWICK
DUMBO
Brooklyn Bridge
High St
Clark St
VINEGAR HILL
Brooklyn-Queens Expwy
Flatbush Ave
Bedford Ave
FORT GREENE
CLINTON HILL
Fulton St
Fulton St
Lafayette Ave
BEDFORD-STUYVESANT
Atlantic Ave
Atlantic Ave
BROOKLYN
YES
PROSPECT HEIGHTS
GOWANUS
Grand Army Plaza
4th Ave
Eastern Pkwy-Brooklyn Museum
CROWN HEIGHTS
PARK SLOPE
Prospect Park W
Flatbush Ave
Prospect Ave
Prospect Park
Prospect Pkwy
15th St-Prospect Park
Prospect Park
GREENWOOD HEIGHTS
0
2 km
0
1 mile

BROOKLYN BRIDGE Park

VIEWS | DINING | LEISURE

Jaw-dropping views, activities, and alfresco restaurants, plus stores and performance spaces: Brooklyn Bridge Park is a one-stop shop for urban leisure. It's all wrapped up in 85 acres of winding paths and piers stretching along the East River, making this recently revived urban oasis the consummate site for a quintessential New York afternoon.

RESUL MUSLU/SHUTTERSTOCK ©

How to

Getting here A/C to High St, 2/3 to Clark St or F to York St. For a grand entrance, walk over the Brooklyn Bridge or take the ferry – boats depart from Midtown's 34th St and FiDi's Pier 11.

When to go The views are great year-round, but the outdoor activities are best from May to October.

Top tip If walking across the Brooklyn Bridge, start early or late to beat crowds.

BRYAN SIERRA12/SHUTTERSTOCK ©

Fulton Ferry Landing

Begin your journey at **Fulton Ferry Landing**, where 19th-century poet Walt Whitman often sailed across the East River. Look at the dock's guard rails and you'll see lines from his 1856 poem 'Crossing the Brooklyn Ferry' engraved.

Like so much of NYC, this landscape has morphed since Whitman wrote '...Brooklyn of ample hills was mine.' In the coming decades, the Brooklyn and Manhattan Bridges became Big Apple landlines. Red brick buildings shot up along the waterfront, home to companies that manufactured goods like cardboard boxes and Brillo pads. Commercial production didn't last long: by the 1970s, businesses left and the waterfront became a wasteland. Industrial facades, cobblestone streets and antique railroad tracks remain, but the

ROMAN BABAKIN/SHUTTERSTOCK ©

Dumbo Detour

Dumbo (Down Under the Manhattan Bridge Overpass) hugs the park's northern stretches – a 25-block dreamscape for shopping and food. The best time for exploration is on weekends between April and December, when **Brooklyn Flea** takes over 80 Pearl St, with vendors selling wares under a giant Manhattan Bridge archway.

Top left Brooklyn Bridge Park **Bottom left** Fulton Ferry Landing **Above** Dumbo waterfront is otherwise transformed – a triumph of urban redesign.

North: Kitschy Thrills & Crowds

Venture north of Fulton Ferry for photogenic East River panoramas and strips of stores. You'll get 360-degree views while spinning around **Jane's Carousel** ($3) – a vintage treasure from 1922 housed in a Pritzker Prize–winning acrylic box. It's come a long way since its days at an Ohio amusement park, with 48 carved horses, two chariots and 1200 dazzling lights.

Behind the carousel is **Empire Stores**, which houses the **Time Out Market** (a collection of food stalls and bars), plus retail chains. To see the scenery from above, head to Time Out Market's 5th-floor terrace.

South: Pretty Piers & Floating Boats

Wander south from Fulton Ferry, and there's a pier for all pleasures. At **Bargemusic**, a

Stroll the Brooklyn Bridge

When this marvel of modern engineering opened in 1883, it was the world's first steel suspension bridge and the first land link between Manhattan and Brooklyn, spanning 1596ft across the East River. Longer NYC bridges have since snatched the spotlight, but the 1-mile-plus journey across the **Brooklyn Bridge** still inspires awe. Its elevated pedestrian path is like an open-air Gothic cathedral. Take the free, breeze-buffeted path for soul-stirring views. The Manhattan entrance is directly off City Hall Park and there are two in Brooklyn – Prospect St and Washington St leads to Dumbo (close to the park); an entrance at Tillary St and Boerum Pl leads to Brooklyn Heights.

Left Kayaking, Pier 2
Below Bargemusic

coffee-bean barge transformed into a performance hall, you can catch classical chamber concerts while rocking to East River waves. Performances are usually Friday to Sunday.

Crowds peter out around **Pier 1**, a collection of green carpets stitching together footpaths, perfect for sunset strolls. From May through September, **Brooklyn Bridge Park Boathouse** (bbpboathouse.org) volunteers hang out at **Pier 2**, offering free 20-minute kayaking sessions (reservations open two weeks in advance).

Sparrows and migrating birds flap around **Pier 3**, with its leafy esplanade and picnic-perfect meadow. Cormorants and ducks paddle around **Pier 4** – a sandy strip lapped by waves.

Crowds pick up around **Pier 6**, particularly in summer when outdoor eating options open. If you want something sweet, grab a scoop of ice cream from **OddFellows** (Pier 5) and find a river-facing bench to admire FiDi's skyscrapers. At **Fornino at Pier 6**, you can order wood-fired pizza, sandwiches and drinks for an unfussy meal at communal picnic tables. Expect a swankier setting at **Pilot** (the western edge of Pier 6), a moored wooden schooner where sun-kissed passengers slurp oysters and cocktails from May to October. The food here is fine, but you're coming for views – they stretch from Lady Liberty to the Empire State Building.

Highway with a View

A COMPLICATED LOOK AT BROOKLYN'S BEST VISTA

New York City's perpetual state of reinvention might be awe-inspiring, but for every skyscraper built or roadway erected, something else meets its demise. This complex reality of urban planning crashes head first on a Brooklyn expressway, where a prized park and a problematic thoroughfare are inextricably intertwined.

Left Brooklyn-Queens Expressway
Centre Brooklyn-Battery Tunnel
Right Brooklyn Heights Promenade

KAROLIS KAVOLELIS/SHUTTERSTOCK ©

Standing on the **Brooklyn Heights Promenade** is a cinematic experience. On one side, Manhattan's modern skyscrapers shine like steely mountains; on the other, elegant townhomes conjure images of 19th-century domesticity. The panorama is so mesmerizing it's possible to forget there's a three-level highway flowing underneath.

This is the Brooklyn-Queens Expressway (BQE), an 11.7-mile thoroughfare stretching from Brooklyn-Battery Tunnel near Red Hook to Grand Central Parkway in Queens. As the road snakes past Brooklyn Heights, it becomes a fantastic feat of urban design, seamlessly blending three tiers of traffic with a peaceful public esplanade.

But Brooklyn Heights Promenade is only 1826ft long. To say the rest of the BQE provides peace of any kind is laughable. The cement river floods into six lanes on either side of the promenade and slices through the borough like a knife, carving Red Hook from Carroll Gardens, dicing Dumbo from downtown Brooklyn, cutting across the heart of Williamsburg, and leaving a gash near Greenpoint.

This massive roadway was part of urban planner Robert Moses's manifesto to drive NYC into what he saw as a car-fueled future. And Moses, who held a laundry list of unelected public offices from 1924 to 1968, seldom hit a red light while pushing his plans toward the finish line.

'You can draw any kind of picture you want on a clean slate and indulge your every whim in the wilderness in laying out a New Delhi, Canberra or Brasilia,' Moses once said, 'but when you operate in an overbuilt metropolis, you have to hack your way with a meat ax.'

Moses was a developer of biblical proportions who parted the city like the Red Sea for his cement machinations.

RICOWDE/GETTY IMAGES ©

PATTI MCCONVILLE/ALAMY STOCK PHOTO ©

Many of his public-works projects are celebrated – like Central Park's zoo, the UN headquarters and arts complex Lincoln Center – and it's nearly impossible to travel around New York without riding his roads. During his tenure, he built at least 416 miles of parkways and seven bridges within New York City alone.

The construction of these roads often meant the destruction of entire communities. Moses displaced roughly a quarter of a million New Yorkers through federally funded 'slum clearance' initiatives, tearing through neighborhoods primarily occupied by poor immigrants and people of color without the power to stand up to a political Goliath.

> The panorama is so mesmerizing it's possible to forget there's a three-level highway flowing underneath.

But when Moses announced a plan to barrel the BQE down Hicks St, Brooklyn Heights' affluent white residents begged him to run it along the East River instead. Although this would lead to waterfront wreckage, it would spare most of the community's historic homes. Columbia Heights residents – who lived along the suggested route – went a step further, asking for a deck over the road to replace private gardens they would lose during construction. Moses agreed, but with one minor adjustment: the private gardens would become a park for the people. In 1950, Brooklyn Heights Promenade opened to the public.

Whether this beloved walkway is a gift from an unlikely Robin Hood or a devious form of highway robbery, one thing remains certain – nothing beats the view.

Brooklyn's Squeaky Wheels

The BQE is crumbling – a bit of poetic justice, considering the roadway is a monument to the thorny legacy of Robert Moses. Decades of salt and moisture have weakened the concrete-steel foundation, along with overweight trucks barrelling across the cantilevered roadway. In 2018, NYC hatched a plan to fix a section under the promenade – which would've meant closing the park for six years. Brooklyn Heights residents once again revved up their engines to fight against the closure and got the idea booted. Officials say a new plan will start construction in 2029. This time, however, the residents get to keep their park.

38 Time Travel in BROOKLYN HEIGHTS

LOCAL LEGENDS | ARCHITECTURE | STROLLING

If the stately townhouses of Brooklyn Heights could talk, they'd tell tales of scandalous pastors and bohemian poets, of filthy-rich merchants and former brothels. This King County enclave is a crowning achievement of historic preservation, with over 600 homes predating the Civil War. Uncover stories of bygone New York by strolling through Brooklyn's oldest neighborhood.

NIKREATES/ALAMY STOCK PHOTO ©

Trip Notes

Getting here Take the 2/3/4/5 or R to Borough Hall and explore on foot.

When to go Day time is best for appreciating architectural details. At dusk, you can occasionally peer into brownstone interiors before residents draw their curtains for the evening. Finish on the Brooklyn Heights Promenade for unobstructed sunset views.

Shop & Eat Don't leave without a walk down main drag Montague St; pop into **L'Appartement 4F** for croissants.

Plymouth Church

From the pulpit of **Plymouth Church** (pictured) in the 1850s and '60s, minister Henry Ward Beecher thundered forth to packed pews with outspoken abolitionist sermons. Beecher opened the church's basement as a station on the Underground Railroad and held mock slave auctions during which the congregation would purchase the freedom of actual slaves.

By Tom Meyers

Tom Meyers is a co-host of the Bowery Boys podcast, covering NYC history. @boweryboysnyc

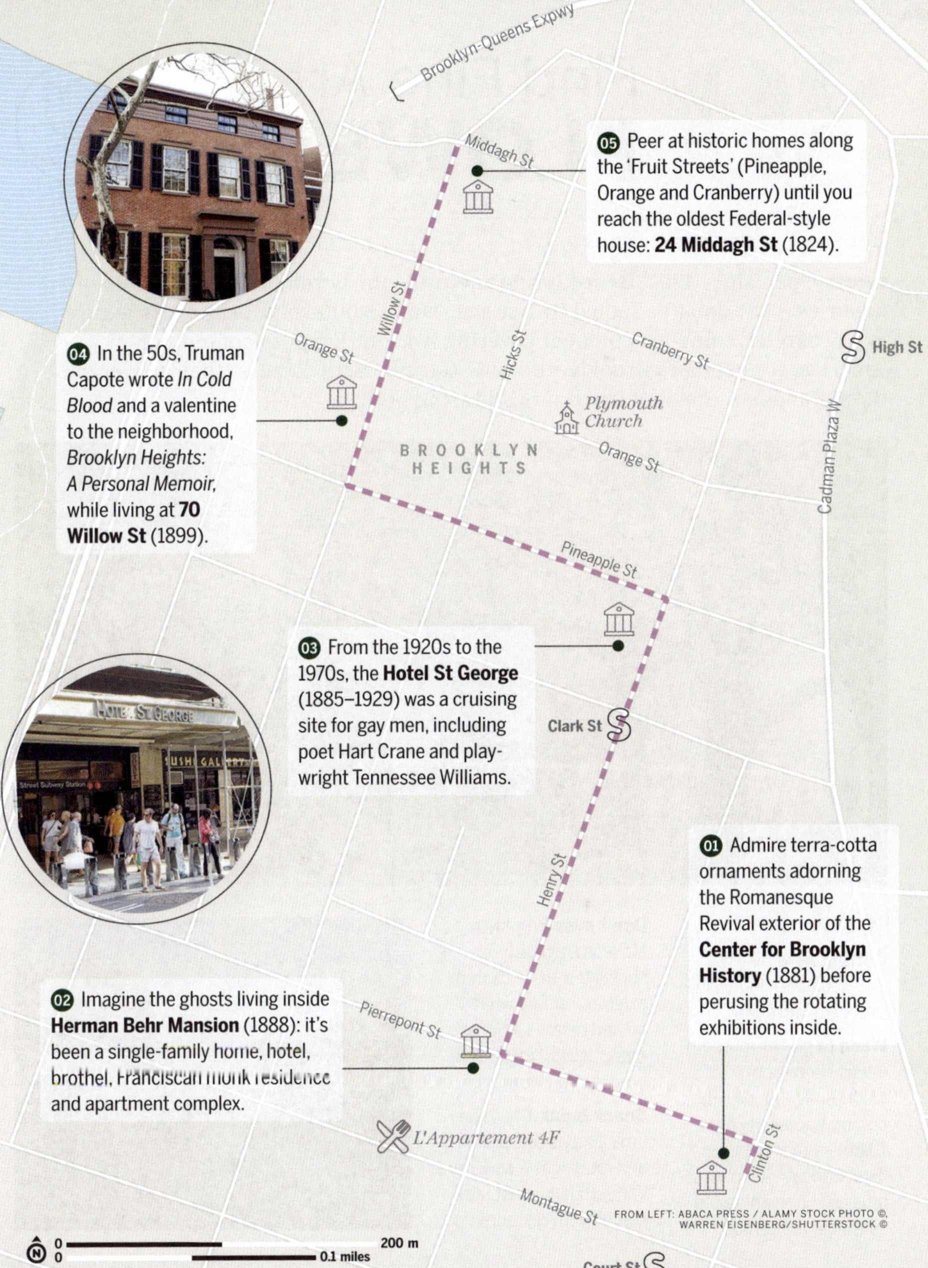

FROM LEFT: ABACA PRESS / ALAMY STOCK PHOTO ©, WARREN EISENBERG/SHUTTERSTOCK ©

39 Find Fine Art & FLOWERS

MUSEUM | BLOSSOMS | PARKS

Open since 1897, **Brooklyn Museum** is the borough's grande dame of art galleries – but don't be fooled by her age. This 56,000-sq-ft, beaux-arts fixture is a progressive fine-arts pioneer covering Ancient Egypt to contemporary America. It neighbors Brooklyn Botanic Garden, with 52 acres that deliver 365 days of blooms. Spend a few hours admiring both.

ANADOLU /GETTY IMAGES ©

How to

Getting here Take the 2/3 to Eastern Parkway–Brooklyn Museum.

When to go The museum opens 11am–6pm Wednesday–Sunday; the botanic garden opens at 10am. Try to stop by for 'First Sunday' at the museums and cherry blossom season at the garden.

Don't miss Brooklyn Museum regularly shows top-tier, ticketed exhibitions. See what's on and reserve a timed-entry ticket if interested. brooklynmuseum.org

Snack break The museum's food is overpriced and mediocre – walk up Vanderbilt Ave instead, loaded with restaurants.

GIRLSEEINGWORLD /SHUTTERSTOCK ©

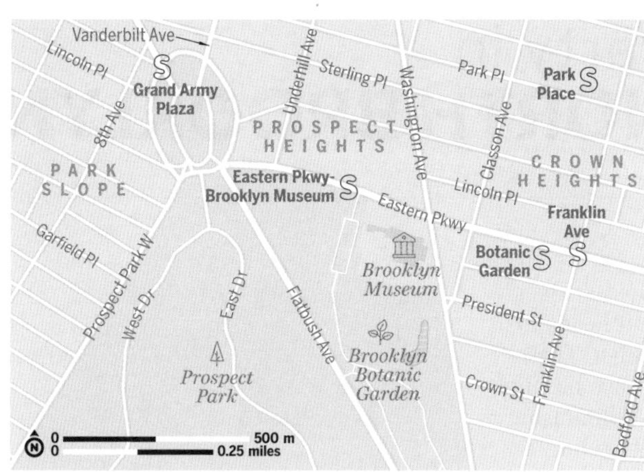

Galleries & Greenery

Celebrate diversity Mainstream museums can feel like shrines to dead white dudes – something Brooklyn Museum is careful to avoid. Work by women gets pride of place on the 4th floor's 8300-sq-ft **Elizabeth Sackler Center for Feminist Art**, including Judy Chicago's 1979 masterpiece, *The Dinner Party*. Walk around the massive triangular dinner table installation to see 39 genitally driven place settings for femme icons like Hatshepsut, the first female pharaoh, Virginia Woolf and more.

The museum's African collection (3rd floor) is equally impressive, chronicling roughly a millennia of artistry through 4500 works.

Visit for stylish Saturdays On the 'First Saturday' of each month, this isn't a regular museum – it's a cool museum. Live music, DJs and artsy activities transform the 1st floor into a house party, with many instalments themed around celebrations like Asian American and Pacific Islander Heritage Month, Black History Month and Pride. Register online and prepare to queue up to get in.

Smell Brooklyn's blooms Due west of the museum is one of three entrances to the beloved **Brooklyn Botanic Garden** (bbg.org/bloom). Tickets cost $18 – well worth it if you've got the hots for horticulture. Crowds pack in around cherry blossom season (April and May) when buds burst on trees around the Japanese Garden and Cherry Esplanade. An annual holiday light show in December is equally popular. Check online for what's in season.

Top left Brooklyn Botanic Garden
Bottom left Prospect Park

Prospect Perfect

Don't tell die-hard Manhattanites: it's understood that landscape architects Frederick Law Olmsted and Calvert Vaux saw Central Park as 'practice' and **Prospect Park**, a 585-acre spread near Brooklyn Museum, as 'perfection.' Their essential elements are similar – you'll find formal features (a concert space; Vaux's architectural touches) along with pastoral pleasures (meadows, groves and lakes). But Prospect Park, designed almost a decade later and opened in 1867, allowed the team to learn from mistakes, creating an uninterrupted bucolic sanctuary where urban sprawl seems like a distant dream. Check out BRIC's summer lineup of concerts at the **Lena Horne Bandshell**, with free and ticketed shows covering multiple genres. bricartsmedia.org

40 Party in NORTH BROOKLYN

CLUBS | DANCING | MUSIC

When the city that doesn't sleep wants to dance until dawn, it heads to a warehouse in North Brooklyn. These once-abandoned buildings have become the prime settings for East Williamsburg and Bushwick's transformation into a global nightlife destination, where all are welcome and anything goes. Join an eccentric set of club kids step-touching toward a liberated tomorrow inside these industrial playgrounds.

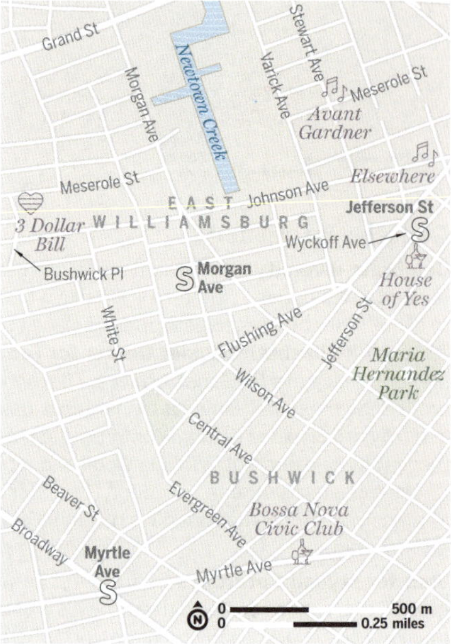

How to

Getting here Take the L to Montrose Ave for East Williamsburg or Jefferson St for Bushwick.

When to go As a general rule, 10pm is too early for the dance floor and 2am is too late.

Plan ahead To ensure admittance, pre-purchase tickets through the Dice or Resident Advisor apps – both fantastic resources for finding parties. Events with well-known DJs regularly sell out. If you can't snag a ticket, try queuing early at the door to get in.

Pick Your Club

Indie jams Sip cocktails on a rooftop as the sun sets over Bushwick before exploring a three-floor maze of music venues below. This is **Elsewhere** (elsewhere.club) – a former furniture factory that hosts indie concerts, dance parties and immersive art shows. The vibe depends on the act. Check the schedule online.

Queer brew 3 Dollar Bill (3dollarbillbk.com), Brooklyn's biggest queer club, throws circuit parties, flea markets and fantastic drag shows. Day parties **Ty Tea** (outdoor pop tunes) and **Motherdisco** offer dance floor liberation.

Glitter explosion An ice factory-turned-arts temple, **House of Yes** (houseofyes.

Top right Elsewhere
Bottom right Brooklyn Mirage

BLOOMBERG/GETTY IMAGES ©

SANTIAGO FELIFE/GETTY IMAGES ©

How to House of Yes

Dress in something that makes you feel fabulous. Wear your most comfortable, badass dancing shoes. Party with a purpose and set a positive intention: your energy can make someone else's night better. Stick around until 3:45am, when the infamous Last Call Pizza announces closing time by dancing around the bar in a pizza suit.

Kae Burke
Kae Burke is the co-founder and creative director at House of Yes. @kaeburke

org) throws radically inclusive themed events; aerialists and burlesque dancers set the mood. This club isn't the kind of place where you wear a T-shirt and jeans unless they're dipped in glitter. Sporting a psychedelic DIY costume is half the fun.

EDM kingdom The 80,000-sq-ft palace that is **Avant Gardner** isn't just a warehouse – it's a techno universe with multiple rooms spread across an entire block. In summer, a central courtyard opens as **Brooklyn Mirage**, a dance-and-concert space.

Cozy corner Overwhelmed by large spaces? Groove at **Bossa Nova Civic Club**, a bar known as 'Techno Cheers,' where DJs play house, disco or hip-hop for regulars.

Listings

BEST OF THE REST

Reservations Required

Lilia $$$

This pasta restaurant in a former auto shop cranks out some of the best handmade noodles in town. Getting a reservation is notoriously tough, understandably – it's carbohydrate heaven.

Laser Wolf $$$

Everything here is a feast: vegetarian appetizers, skewers cooked over an open fire, plus views of Manhattan – an eye-full from the Hoxton Hotel's terrace.

International Eats & Pizza

Bunna Cafe $$

Forget utensils at this veggie Ethiopian restaurant. Dollops of stewed greens, red lentils and more are scooped by hand with tangy *injera* (a sourdough pancake). Order the 'feast.'

Win Son Bakery $

Pastries like mochi donuts and date cakes and breakfast sandwiches (the veggie milk bun) attract morning lines. Burgers and fried chicken make a good case for returning around dinner.

Bonnie's $$

It's a Cantonese-American marriage, merging things like cacio e pepe with fermented beancurd. It's also a raucous wedding party, serving super-strong Long Island iced tea pots with eight servings each.

Ops $$

Grab a table in the rustic-chic interior, order a glass of natural wine then scarf down sourdough Neapolitan pies straight from the wood-burning oven. Try anything with house-made mozzarella.

Classy Cocktails & Wine

Four Horsemen $$$

LCD Soundsystem frontman James Murphy is the owner behind this Michelin-starred natural wine bar with an exceptional food menu. Order half glasses to take advantage of the extensive collection.

Maison Premiere $$$

Visiting the green fairy at this oyster-and-cocktail bar is like traveling to 19th-century New Orleans. Absinthe flows from a marble fountain; soft jazz bounces off fleur-de-lis adorned walls.

Long Island Bar $$

Slide into a red vinyl booth at this cool-cat juice joint from 1951. With cocktails crafted by Cosmo inventor Toby Cecchini, it's no wonder hip locals still keep this Cobble Hill bar-and-restaurant abuzz.

Craft Beer in North Brooklyn

Talea $$

New York's first women-owned brewery opened in 2021 and quickly became a city-wide chain. Head to the original Williamsburg location for fruit-forward beers in the pastel-tiled interior.

Grimm Artisanal Ales $$

It's nearly impossible to decide between the experimental IPAs, barrel-aged sours and chocolatey lagers at this East Williamsburg operation, so order a flight and sample them all.

Coffee & Confections

SEY Coffee $

If good coffee is like fine wine, the baristas at this Nordic-style roaster are some of the city's top sommeliers. SEY's mad-scientist attention to detail ensures impeccable brews.

Devoción $

Sip Colombian coffee while lounging on a tufted leather sofa in this local chain's industrial Williamsburg location. There's plenty of seating, yet this stylish space always seems packed.

Poppy's $

Early birds get the egg galettes at this quaint cafe, but late risers are still in luck. Fresh-made sandwiches and a case of delectable sweets never disappoint.

Williamsburg's Specialty Stores

Quimby's

You could spend an hour inside this renegade word den leafing through boxes stuffed with locally made zines. Subjects cover everything from *Barbie*'s queer subtext to Aleister Crowley's unforgettable quotes.

DS & Durga

Travel the world on an olfactory tour through this Brooklyn-born fragrance shop. Explore California with Big Sur After Rain or keep it local with Wild Brooklyn Lavender.

Heatonist

Williamsburg's artisanal hot sauce store doesn't make you guess if the 'extreme warning' on labels like Psycho Hot Sauce are serious. Just sample them at the tasting bar.

Performing Arts & Museums

City Reliquary

Walk through an antique subway turnstile into this tiny Williamsburg museum dedicated

Brooklyn Academy of Music

OSUGI/SHUTTERSTOCK ©

to an oddball mix of Big Apple ephemera, including Lady Liberty figurines and a shrine to Brooklyn Dodgers star Jackie Robinson.

Brooklyn Academy of Music

BAM is the cultural heart of Kings County with multiple venues showcasing a mix of groundbreaking plays, revered dance troupes, classical operas and indie films.

Fabulous Markets & Festivals

Smorgasburg

Every Saturday from April to October foodies file into Marsha P Johnson State Park to sample an array of handheld treats at this open-air culinary bazaar featuring local vendors.

Soul Summit Music Festival

Hang with hip locals in Fort Greene Park on summer Sunday afternoons during this free jamboree with house music DJs, food stands and fashion vendors.

Bushwick Collective Block Party

World renowned muralists paint Bushwick walls in the days leading up to this June celebration with food and live music. See street art year-round by walking along Jefferson and Troutman Sts between Cypress and Knickerbocker Aves.

DAY TRIPS

ART | NATURE | RECREATION

DAY TRIPS
Trip Builder

TAKE YOUR PICK OF MUST-SEES AND HIDDEN GEMS

One of NYC's greatest attributes is its proximity to destinations that feel worlds apart. Rugged mountains are but an hour away and buzzy beaches are practically next door. When the city that doesn't sleep leaves you in need of a recharge, these idyllic excursions make for energizing escapes.

Day Trip Notes

Best for Cultured enclaves, lively beaches and mountain landscapes

Getting around Public transportation – including Metro-North and NJ Transit – makes getting out of the city easy and affordable. Car rentals are expensive, but they can be beneficial for getting off the beaten path.

Tip Plan ahead for summer trips, particularly in July and August. New Yorkers are notorious for booking up the best hotels, restaurants and excursions months in advance.

Climb the Hudson Highlands on an arduous hike to **Breakneck Ridge** (p197).
1½ hours by train
Hike between mountains and museums in the charming town of **Beacon** (p198).
1½ hours by train
CONNECTICUT
Bridgeport
Norwalk
Hudson River
Stamford
Greenwich
Long Island Sound
New Rochelle
Yonkers
Mt Vernon
NEW YORK
Long Island
Brentwood
Levittown
Hempstead
Fire Island National Seashore
The Pines
Gateway National Recreation Area
Long Beach
Ride the century-old wooden Cyclone for a summer thrill at **Coney Island** (p200).
1hr from Midtown
ASTROLAND
CYCLONE
ATLANTIC OCEAN
Strut down **Asbury Park's** (p204) historic beachfront boardwalk along the Jersey Shore.
1½ hours by train
0
50 km
0
25 miles

41 Storm King ART CENTER

SCULPTURES | WILDLIFE | MOUNTAINS

Hike around the Hudson Valley's rolling hills at this pastoral art park located 60 miles north of New York City. Mammoth-sized sculptures sprout from Storm King's 500 acres of well-groomed woodlands and meadows, blurring the line between human handiwork and mother nature. Scope out the scenery in autumn, when the surrounding forests put on an art show worthy of their own exhibition.

365 FOCUS PHOTOGRAPHY/SHUTTERSTOCK ©

How to

Getting here Driving is best if you want to explore areas surrounding the center (one hour from Midtown). By train, take the Metro-North Hudson Line from Grand Central to Beacon, from where Storm King provides round-trip shuttle services on weekends. Coach USA offers direct bus service from Port Authority.

When to go Open early April to mid-December. Each season provides a unique canvas for the collection.

Top tips Pack a picnic, dress for the weather and wear comfortable shoes.

CHOONGKY/SHUTTERSTOCK ©

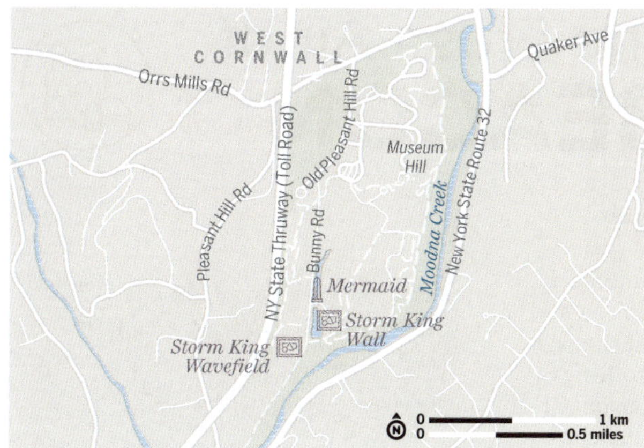

Top left Storm King Art Center
Bottom left Breakneck Ridge

Earthy Exhibits

Panoramic peak Climb to the top of **Museum Hill**, the center's highest plateau, to enjoy expansive views and see the bulk of the center's offerings. A restored French Normandy-style chateau, built in 1935, serves as a gallery space and museum shop. Ionic columns from a 19th-century mansion frame nearby **Schunnemunk Mountain**.

Site-specific art Seek out sublime sculptures that intentionally interact with the landscape. Get swept away in Maya Lin's *Storm King Wavefield,* an 11-acre earthwork of hills that undulate like the Hudson Highlands. Lose yourself in the passing clouds reflected in Sarah Sze's *Fallen Sky,* a ground-bound, 36ft-wide sphere made of stainless steel. Follow Andy Goldsworthy's 2278ft-long *Storm King Wall* as it snakes through trees, slips into a pond and makes a mad dash for the property's edge.

Local flora & fauna Stay vigilant while ambling along native grasslands, creeks and allées to spot deer, box turtles and cottontail rabbits. Canadian geese have an affinity for the weeping willows surrounding Roy Lichtenstein's *Mermaid* and 80 other bird species can be seen soaring throughout the park.

Fall foliage Summer's verdant forests become a riot of reds, yellows and oranges between mid-September and mid October, the prime time for regional leaf displays. Consult I Love NY's fall foliage map to plan a peak-season trip (iloveny.com).

Wheel around Zip through the park quickly by renting a bicycle ($20–30) or hopping on the wheelchair-accessible tram loop.

Nearby Art & Trails

Storm King is a stone's throw from rewarding hikes and stylish hamlets like Beacon (p198). Tack on one or two of these stops for a weekend affair in the Hudson Valley.

Storm King Mountain Storm King Art Center's name comes from this 1300ft mound a few miles east. A 2.4-mile hiking loop circles its crown with river and mountain views.

Boscobel House and Gardens This 19th-century Federalist home, overlooking the Hudson River near Beacon, showcases the style of fledgling Americans still tethered to British influence.

Breakneck Ridge Brace yourself for rocky scrambles and steep ascents on this strenuous 3.2-mile hike, accessible on summer weekends via Metro-North.

42 The Fresh Air of BEACON

MUSEUMS | HIKING | SHOPPING

Bohemian Beacon's unofficial nickname is 'Brooklyn North' – a nod to ex-urbanites who've spent the past 20 years transforming it into Kings County's scrappy upstate cousin. All the Brooklyn-as-brand signifiers are on Main St: artisanal boutiques, small-batch breweries and avant-garde art galleries. Unlike NYC, however, the town abuts the Hudson Highlands, where urbanites break in their hiking boots.

How to

Getting here Beacon is 60 miles north of NYC – a 1½-hour train ride from Grand Central via Metro-North and a similarly long drive from Midtown. The train station is a 15-minute walk from Main St; the Beacon Free Loop bus travels from the train station to Main St from Monday through Saturday.

When to go Weekends are best, when all Main St shops are open.

Top tip Pair a Beacon trip with Storm King for a full weekend adventure.

Paintings, Pints & Peaks

Mega-sized minimalism

Most Manhattan day trippers who arrive via Metro-North head straight to **Dia Beacon** to drool over NYC's most sought-after commodity – space. This 300,000-sq-ft former Nabisco printing factory devotes itself to minimalist paintings and massive sculptures. The most transportive works feel less 'contemporary art museum' and more 'aesthete's playground,' like Richard Serra's rust-red *Torqued Ellipses*. Circling his steel sculptures is akin to hiking Arizona's Antelope Canyon. Free guided tours take place at noon and 1:30pm on Saturday and Sunday, though it's best

Top right Store, Beacon
Bottom right Dia Beacon

BARRY WINIKER /GETTY IMAGES ©

MAURITIUS IMAGES GMBH/ALAMY STOCK PHOTO ©

Does Anyone Still Wear a Hat?

Before Fishkill Creek became Beacon's prized recreational ribbon, it was the powerhouse behind the city's most popular export – hats. Matteawan Manufacturing Company started the trend in 1864, followed by Tioronda Hat Works in 1879 and roughly 50 more companies in coming years. Most set up shop creekside, using the water to clean and dye wool – until cheap imports and the Great Depression decimated the industry. Many companies abandoned their factories in the 20th century.

to experience the museum at your own pace.

Main St stroll Next stop is Main St, with its mile-long stretch of restaurants, cafes, boutiques and breweries. Pop into **Noble Pies** for a slice of apple-y Americana or save your appetite for **Homespun Foods** – a colorful retro kitchen serving brunch and lunch classics. Walk off your meal en route to **Hudson Valley Brewery**, where funky ales get made in-house.

High peaks One of the best things to do around Beacon is hike. **Mt Beacon** is a 4-mile out-and-back journey passing charred hotel ruins on the way to a fire tower with great views. Budget three hours.

43 Coney ISLAND

ECCENTRIC | NOSTALGIC | THRILLING

Walk down Coney Island's boardwalk on a sweltering day and you'll see a mix of well-known kitschy icons. Tattooed mermaids, vintage roller coasters and greasy food stands have greeted a sea of New Yorkers since the 19th century. But visit during one of Coney Island's annual festivals and you'll see something unique – the faded glamour of Brooklyn's 'riviera' returned to its former glory.

GARY HERSHORN/GETTY IMAGES ©

How to

Getting here Take the F/D or N/Q to Coney Island-Stillwell Ave. Budget one hour from Midtown Manhattan.

When to go The biggest festivals happen in June, July and January. Visit between Memorial Day and Labor Day when beaches and amusement parks open. The boardwalk is open year-round.

Ride passes Coney Island has two main amusement parks and they require separate entrance fees: **Deno's Wonder Wheel Park** and **Luna Park**, which has most of the rides.

STEVE EDREFF /SHUTTERSTOCK ©

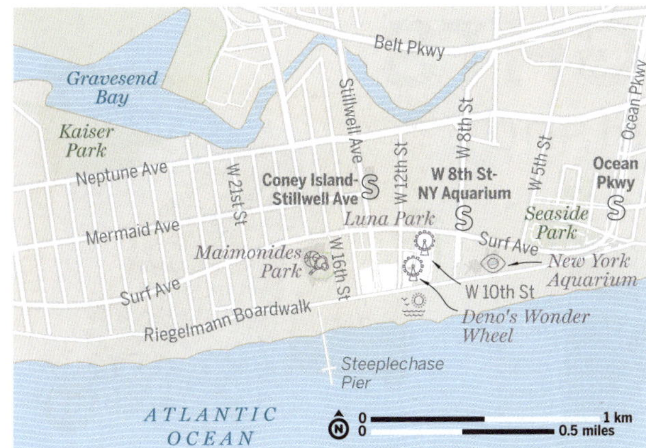

Find Your Festival

Mermaid Parade Sirens of the sea trade their fins for feet at the Mermaid Parade, an annual summer solstice celebration started in 1983. Ariel fans beware: this gritty festival isn't a Disney sing-along – it's an offbeat explosion of artistic expression that skews more Mardi Gras than Mickey Mouse. Blend in with the crowds along Surf Ave to see homemade floats, or don your craziest nautical fashions to compete in the best-dressed competition. Glitter, body paint and an open mind are all that's required to win.

Hot-dog eating contest Join thousands of strong-stomached spectators on the corner of Stillwell and Surf every Fourth of July to watch **Nathan's Famous Hot Dog Eating Contest**. The annual spectacle pits wiener-eating wizards against one another in a battle to see who downs the most dogs in 10 minutes. The first recorded event occurred in 1972, but legend says the tradition dates to 1916, when Nathan Handwerker established the business. Make it an all-day affair and stick around for fireworks, which light the night sky from **Steeplechase Park**.

Polar bear plunge Wash away last year's woes by plunging into the icy Atlantic with the **Coney Island Polar Bear Club**, founded in 1903. Every 1 January, thousands of New Yorkers join the warm-blooded crew near Coney Island's boardwalk for a refreshing start to the new year.

Top left Deno's Wonder Wheel Park
Bottom left Mermaid Parade

Tips from the Mayor

For mermaids Hip Brooklyn parents use the Mermaid Parade for sex education, but consider staying home if you're a little bit prudish.

For wieners If you get inspired to run your own hot-dog-eating contest, dunk the bun in a cup of water and swish the hot dog casing in your hand. It'll save you lots of time and effort.

For polar bears That part of the body men are afraid will shrink isn't the problem. The real problem is that your toes will be numb for hours afterward. Wear into the ocean a pair of shoes you don't mind ruining.

Dick Zigun

Dick Zigun, the unofficial 'Mayor' of Coney Island, is the founder and artistic director of Coney Island USA. X: @dickzigun

THE SIGHTS
of Coney Island

01 Walk the waterfront
Riegelmann Boardwalk, a 2.5-mile wood-plank walkway dating back to 1923, serves as the main thoroughfare between the beach and the rides.

02 The Funny Face
The excessively toothy grin of Tillie, once the logo for the now-demolished Steeplechase Park, is an everlasting symbol of Coney Island quirk.

03 Brave the Cyclone
Thrill-seekers started screaming from the seats of this rickety wooden roller coaster when it took its first 85ft plunge in 1927.

04 Nathan's Famous Franks
In 1916 Polish immigrant Nathan Handwerker started hawking his now-famous hot dogs for a nickel on the corner of Surf and Stillwell.

05 The Thunderbolt
This 2234ft-long coaster whirls passengers around at 56mph.

06 Deep Sea Diving
Wander through the New York Aquarium's coral reef tunnel to see black-tip reef sharks and over 100 other marine species.

07 Coney's Oldest Attraction
Sweeping views of the Jersey Shore and Manhattan appear while spinning around the 1920 Wonder Wheel.

08 Sizzling Slice
Get in line for a thin-crust slice of Neapolitan pizza from Totonno's, open since 1921.

09 Brooklyn's Eiffel Tower
Stand underneath the defunct Parachute Jump, a 250ft-tall landmark designed for the 1939 New York World's Fair and relocated here in 1941.

10 Beach Baseball
Enjoy ocean views while watching the minor-league Brooklyn Cyclones play ball at Maimonides Park.

11 See a Sideshow
A sword swallower and a fire eater are just a couple of the weird and wonderful acts in the Coney Island Circus Sideshow.

12 Gone fishing
Rough-and-tumble fishers from all walks of life set up their poles along Steeplechase Pier to wait for the next big catch.

44 The Jersey SHORE

BEACH | MUSIC | LEGACY

Artsy and edgy Asbury Park is the Jersey Shore's revitalized jewel – a once-derelict haunt amid a bohemian rebirth. New-wave eateries, boutique shopping and a thriving music scene attract a diverse crowd of city slickers, big families and LGBTIQ+ folks to what's recently become a postcard-perfect summertime escape. Mosey along the historic seaside boardwalk at the center of the renaissance.

How to

Getting here New Jersey Transit provides direct train service from Penn Station to Asbury Park. The Seastreak Ferry (seastreak.com) is a scenic but more expensive alternative docking in Highlands, located 30 minutes north by cab. Budget 1½ to two hours if driving.

When to go This is a heavily trafficked summer town. Visit in late spring or early autumn to beat crowds.

Top tip Purchase mandatory beach passes at the beach office or via apbeachpasses.com ($6 weekdays, $10 weekends and holidays).

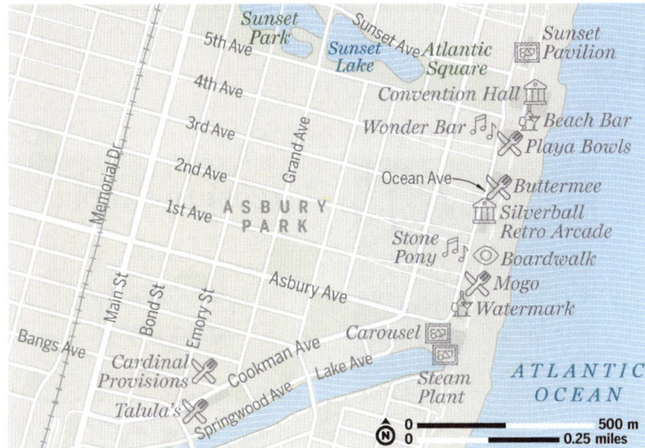

Boardwalk & Beyond

Time travel Imagine *Gatsby*-era glam while strolling along the seashore. Start by passing through the **Convention Hall**, built between 1928 and 1930 by the same architects behind NYC's Grand Central Terminal. Retired pinball wizards can rediscover their youth at the **Silverball Retro Arcade** by playing games that date back to the 1930s. To the south, a gutted beaux-arts casino and carousel stand as ghostly reminders of the town's Jazz Age heyday.

Dine and drink Asbury Park's mile-long boardwalk is an epicurean delight packed with creative food stalls. Try Korean-fusion tacos at **Mogo**, bite into mini pancakes from **Buttermee**, or cool down with a fruit smoothie from **Playa Bowls**. Chug rum bowls at **Beach Bar**, mere steps from the sand, or sit on the **Watermark**'s sizable seaside deck for a classy moonlit cocktail hour. If you've got a car, there's more to eat around Cookman St. Stop by **Cardinal Provisions** for breakfast and **Talula's** for pizza.

Rock out Music reigns supreme in Asbury Park, and Bruce Springsteen is the scene's favorite son. Follow his path to fame by heading to the **Stone Pony** (stoneponyonline.com), a boardwalk-adjacent rock club where he got his start in the 1970s. Check the venue's Summer Stage schedule to see big-name acts perform under the stars. There's also **Wonder Bar** (wonderbarasburypark.com), with the silly-sinister Tillie face painted out front, where up-and-coming talent blast rock, pop and punk.

Top left Asbury Park
Bottom left Wonder Bar

Seaside Street Art

The **Wooden Walls Project** beautifies Asbury Park's boardwalk with murals created by prominent street artists. See founder Jenn Hampton's favorite pieces at these spots:

Sunset Pavilion Rubin-45's *7800° Fahrenheit* includes three panels with geometric designs.

Carousel The circular floor mural by local artist Porkchop reads 'Good Thoughts, Good Words, Good Deeds' in five languages.

Steam Plant Ann Lewis' *Never Turn Your Back on the Ocean* is a 50ft mural in the windows of an inactive power plant.

Jenn Hampton
Jenn Hampton is the curator of the Wooden Walls Project and Parlor Gallery. She lives in Asbury Park, NJ. @woodenwallsproject

Practicalities

Right Little Island (p83) and the West Village

EASY STEPS FROM THE AIRPORT TO THE CITY CENTRE

Most visitors arrive in NYC via one of three airports. Flights to John F Kennedy (JFK) and LaGuardia (LGA) land in Queens, while Newark (EWR) lands in New Jersey, accessible to NYC via the New Jersey Transit train line. Depending on your route, you might arrive by bus at Port Authority or on a train at Grand Central Terminal or Penn Station.

AT THE AIRPORT

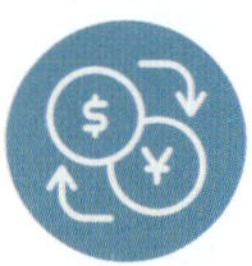

CURRENCY EXCHANGE
Currency exchange booths are located at various terminals before exiting airports, but transaction fees are often high. Your best bet is to take out money from an airport ATM, where you can get US cash with an accepted debit or credit card.

TAXIS
Grabbing a cab from the airport to Manhattan is efficient if it's late at night or early in the morning, but if you land around rush hour, opt for public transportation. Travel time will be similar and you'll save $70 or more.

F11PHOTO/SHUTTERSTOCK ©

SIM CARDS You can purchase prepaid SIM cards at airport retail stores, but they'll be cheaper at cellular stores outside the airport.

WI-FI Wi-fi is free throughout all airports. It can occasionally be slow. If you need reliable high-speed, try an airline lounge.

VISAS Foreign visitors to the US must obtain a visa unless they are from a country that qualifies for the visa waiver program.

Rideshare Keen on taking a car from the airport to the city center? Ensure you're hopping in a certified cab, Uber or Lyft. You may be greeted by friendly faces offering rides without the hassle of waiting in the taxi line, but don't fall for it: these are scammers who charge exorbitant prices. Follow signs for designated taxi pick-up spots.

GETTING TO THE CITY CENTER

JFK Driving from JFK to Midtown takes 30 to 45 minutes, traffic pending. Cabs cost $70 before surcharges and tips. Public transportation is cheaper: hop on the AirTrain ($8.50) and take the LIRR to 34th St-Penn station (30 to 45 minutes, $18.75), the A from Howard Beach or the E from Jamaica (one to 1½ hours, $2.90).

LGA Cabs from LGA to Midtown cost between $30 and $40, excluding tolls and tip. For public transit, take the free LaGuardia Link Q70 shuttle to subways in Jackson Heights ($2.90). The M60 SBS bus connects to A/C, B/D, 1/2/3 and 4/5 trains. Budget 50 to 90 minutes.

HOW MUCH FOR A...

Avoid the Shuttle Shuttle vans from airports to Midtown cost more than other forms of public transit and can get stuck in gnarly traffic. Don't try it.

Train or Subway While subway rides are the cheapest option for transportation, trains are more comfortable and efficient. Download the NJ Transit and MTA apps to pre-purchase tickets.

EWR to NYC If you're landing at EWR, travel to Manhattan by train: take the Newark AirTrain ($8) to the Newark airport train station, then catch the NJ Transit train to Penn Station (roughly one hour, $16). The Newark Airport Express shuttle bus service also serves Manhattan ($18). Cabs often cost upwards of $50.

OTHER POINTS OF ENTRY

Grand Central Terminal If you're traveling within New York State or somewhere nearby, Metro-North Railroad and Long Island Railroad trains stop at this gorgeous Midtown landmark and transportation center, with easy access to buses, taxis and the 4/5/6, 7 and S subway lines. Stick around a while – you'll find great dining options throughout (p108).

Penn Station Amtrak, Long Island Railroad and NJ Transit trains stop at this Midtown hub, recently renovated to include the exquisite Moynihan Train Hall – a worthwhile visit, even if you aren't arriving by locomotive. 1/2/3 trains stop directly at Penn Station.

Port Authority Bus Terminal The country's largest bus terminal serves 7000 buses on an average day, with all major carriers represented. The area (near Times Square) gets sketchy – try not to linger.

Manhattan Cruise Terminal Most cruise ships will port at this Hudson River dock a few avenues from Times Square. If you port at the Brooklyn Cruise Terminal in Red Hook, don't head straight to Manhattan – you're at the ideal jumping-off point for exploring Brooklyn's beautiful brownstone neighborhoods.

Car Avoid driving. Traffic is hectic, parking is a nightmare and bridge tolls add up quickly.

TRANSPORTATION TIPS TO HELP YOU GET AROUND

Transportation in NYC is more than yellow cabs and subway cars, though both are icons of urban commuting. Appreciate the city's shifting landscape while zipping by on bikes, boats and buses, or join the sidewalk ballet by hoofing it block-by-block. It might seem like chaos at first, but New York's choreography is precise.

Subway ride $2.90

Citi Bike Day Pass $19

NYC Ferry $4

BICYCLE

Renting a set of wheels is a fast, fun way to explore. Try Citi Bike, NYC's bikeshare program. Follow traffic laws. Stick to protected bike lanes.

TRAM

The aerial tramway linking Manhattan to Roosevelt Island provides a cinematic path across the East River, showcasing city panoramas for the price of a subway ride.

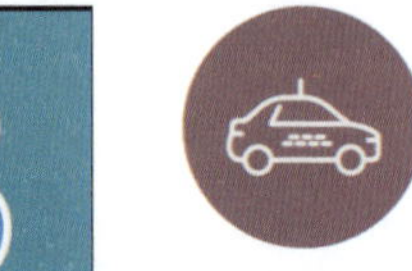

TAXI

When the taxi's top light is lit, it's available. Step off the curb and throw your arm in the air. Alternatively, use the Curb app.

RIDESHARE

Ridesharing apps Uber and Lyft are easy to use and safe but subject to surge pricing. The cost of rides can be inconsistent.

FERRY

Riding a boat doesn't always make sense, but it's usually a magical experience. The free Staten Island ferry is a joy ride disguised as public transportation.

BUS

In Manhattan, bus routes run north to south or east to west – ideal for short distances, traveling across town or for folks who have difficulty using stairs.

HELPFUL APPS Google Maps is the ubiquitous NYC navigation tool, though CityMapper shows even more transportation options. Subway Time tells you when the next subway arrives.

PUBLIC TRANSPORTATION ACCESSIBILITY

For wheelchair users, the easiest way to get around is on buses, which come equipped with wheelchair lifts and wheelchair-reserved seating. Trains are tough – only 25% have accessible elevators and aren't always operational (check new.mta.info/accessibility/stations). Taxis can accommodate manual and power wheelchairs. Order accessible cabs on the Curb app.

TIPS FOR THE SUBWAY

Taking the train might seem daunting but it also provides a dynamic snapshot of New York. Movie stars, mariachi bands, drag queens and school children all commute underground. Follow these tips to ride like a pro.

Navigation Trains run in two directions – ensure you know which direction you're going before hopping on.

Local & express Most lines have both local and express trains. Local trains stop at all stations (black dots on subway maps), while express stations skip stops (stopping at white dots on subway maps). Common mistake: hopping on an express train and skipping one's intended destination. Subway schedules often change on weekends – remain alert.

Payment Use OMNY, a contactless payment system, to purchase subway and bus rides operated

by the Metropolitan Transit Authority (MTA). No need to download an app – just tap a contactless credit or debit card connected to your smart device. Pay for 12 rides using the same card within seven days; additional rides within the week are free. You can also use an OMNY card, available at station kiosks.

Subway dos Always give up seats for people who are disabled, elderly or pregnant. If the subway is crowded and you're wearing a backpack, take it off and hold it in front of you so it doesn't hit other passengers. If you're sitting down, keep your legs together (no manspreading) – and keep your feet underneath you to avoid tripping people passing by.

Subway don'ts Don't get into that empty car – there's often a very stinky reason why no one else is inside. Don't engage with aggressive riders (including making eye contact); if something makes you uncomfortable, change cars at the next stop.

UNIQUE AND LOCAL WAYS TO STAY

Every New York neighborhood is a city unto itself. Choose a home base packed with the elements you admire most. While many NYC hotels are expensive and tiny, there are still some boutique budget options and a smattering of decent hostels. Home shares from sites like Airbnb are difficult to find.

HOW MUCH FOR A NIGHT IN...

Hostel dorm bed **from $120**

Brooklyn boutique hotel **from $300**

Manhattan luxury hotel **from $800**

LUXURY HOTELS

There's no shortage of high-end, top-dollar accommodations – and even if you're not splurging on an overnight stay, you can usually enjoy their on-site restaurants. Try Italian spot **Locanda Verde** in FiDi's **Greenwich Hotel** and the swanky **Lobby Bar** inside **Dime Square's Nine Orchard**.

MIDRANGE HOTEL

If you don't want to break the bank but still want something classy, consider Downtown Brooklyn's **Ace Hotel** (walkable to Brooklyn Heights and Dumbo) or **Public Hotel**, a Lower East Side spot from Studio 54 co-founder Ian Schrager.

BUDGET HOTELS

Going cheap doesn't mean forgoing style. The West Village's **Jane Hotel** houses guests inside ship-style rooms initially constructed for sailors in 1908. At Flatiron's arty **Freehand**, bunk four to a room to save bucks.

AIRBNBS & APARTMENTS

In 2023 city officials implemented a law prohibiting rentals under 30 days when a host isn't present on the property. Roughly 80% of NYC's Airbnb units immediately vanished; finding one is challenging.

BOOKING

New York's high season is summer (late May to early September) and around the holidays (November through December). Plan ahead – hotel prices reach their peak and finding last-minute accommodations is tough. Prices drop from January through March, though you'll still see premiums for holiday weekends like St Patrick's Day. Consider booking directly with hotels for better rates – third-party sites usually charge service fees. Finding the perfect hotel can be overwhelming – consult the NYC Tourism (nycgo.com/hotels) website for listings.

HOSTELS

Bare bones isn't bad at **HI New York City Hostel** – a super-cheap, clean Upper West Side spot, perfect for young upstarts looking to make travel buddies.

WHERE TO STAY, IF YOU LOVE...

Massive monuments & soaring skyscrapers Lower Manhattan & New York Harbor (p32) From One World Trade Center's gleaming tip to Lady Liberty's shining torch, staying downtown will immerse you in NYC's legacy.

Fashion, food & creativity SoHo, Chinatown, Nolita & Little Italy (p46) Pricey boutiques and galleries pack SoHo and Nolita; dumpling dens and pasta spots cram streets throughout Chinatown and Little Italy.

Innovative style & offbeat edge East Village & the Lower East Side (p62) Old-school immigrant eateries, grungy nightclubs, neat boutiques, captivating museums and vestiges of a seedy punk past.

↓ Architecture, art & urban parks West Village & Chelsea (p78) The modernist High Line park compliments contemporary art spaces like the Whitney during the day. Theater, jazz and LGBTIQ+ bars shine at night.

Bright lights, tall towers & Broadway Midtown (p98) Skyscrapers like the Empire State Building shoot above pulsing Time Square's neon billboards and the Theater District's kicking chorus lines.

↑ World-class museums & mansions Upper East Side (p116) Palace-sized apartments attract modern-day Astors, while Fifth Ave's astounding collection of museums are magnets for all. A touch reserved; always elegant.

Sprawling green spaces & culture Upper West Side (p132) The American Museum of Natural History and Lincoln Center sit between zen escape pads Central and Riverside Parks.

Soulful history & cuisine Harlem (p148) The birthplace of a 1920s renaissance led by African American artists still pulses with the beat of African American culture.

International eats & arts Queens (p162) This enormous, working-class borough exemplifies NYC's image as a global melting pot: eat around the world in Jackson Heights and admire Astoria's artistic expression.

Waterfront views, nightlife & trendsetters Brooklyn (p176) Brooklyn Bridge Park's waterfront footpaths, Williamsburg's lively restaurants and Bushwick's warehouse dance raves – a universe unto itself.

Previous page Jane Hotel **Left** The High Line (p84), Chelsea **Above** Upper East Side (p116)

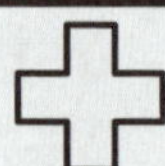

SAFE TRAVEL

NYC is one of the USA's safest cities, but a little common sense goes a long way. Remain alert on subways and streets, dress for the weather (sweltering summers, frigid winters), never leave personal items unattended and always trust your gut.

PEDESTRIAN CROSSING Crosswalk lights may seem like mere suggestions for New Yorkers, but always look both ways before crossing the street – even if it's one-way. E-bikes will often zoom by from seemingly nowhere.

MARIJUANA & ALCOHOL Adults 21 and over can legally use marijuana. Don't smoke in public parks – it's illegal. Drinking from open alcohol containers is also prohibited in public places like parks – though people often do it discreetly.

SUBWAY SAFETY While waiting for the subway, stand away from the platform edge – especially when trains enter or leave the station. Trains are generally safe 24/7, but consider a cab if it's after midnight and you're alone.

Public restrooms are shamefully scarce. Reliable spots include parks, public libraries and transportation hubs (Grand Central, Penn Station). Follow @got2gonyc for filmed reviews of public toilets plus a Google Maps list with over 2000 bathrooms.

ERICK C FREITAS/SHUTTERSTOCK ©

RBLFMR/SHUTTERSTOCK ©

INSURANCE & MEDICATIONS

If you're a foreign visitor, consider buying travel insurance. Medical care and prescription drugs can be expensive in the US – and emergency room visits can cost thousands of dollars. For quick doctor visits, try Urgent Care (without insurance costs are $200-plus). Head to a pharmacy like Duane Reade, CVS or Walgreens for over-the-counter medications.

QUICK TIPS TO HELP YOU MANAGE YOUR MONEY

CASH OR CREDIT? It's best to carry a little bit of cash along with a credit card. Some businesses – especially street vendors and mom-and-pop restaurants – only accept cash, while new businesses are increasingly card-only. ATMs are available at airports, banks, bodegas and smoke shops. Some smaller establishments don't accept $100 bills – carry $20s.

PEDICABS PROBLEMS
Pedicabs solicit tourists with the promise of quick trips at affordable prices, but they charge by the minute and it adds up quickly.

TAX TOWN
NYC is the most expensive city in the US. On top of having one the nation's highest sales tax (8.875%), housing expenses are 4.8% times the national average. Budget accordingly.

CURRENCY

US dollar

HOW MUCH FOR A...

Bodega BEC
$4.50–6

Craft cocktail
$16–22

Broadway show
$20–250

DISCOUNT CARDS CityPASS (citypass.com) offers museum discounts. Buy admission to three to five major tourist attractions and save around 40% on prices – just ensure you want to see what's offered.

PAY WHAT YOU CAN

If the entry fee for a museum is 'pay-what-you-wish,' it means exactly that – pay whatever you desire, no questions asked. If you make an advance reservation online, however, you'll usually have to pony up the suggested fee. Spontaneity can work in your favor: show up sans reservation to save some dough.

DO IT FOR CHEAP NYC gets a bad rep for being unaffordable, but there are plenty of ways to have fun without spending money. You can ride across New York Harbor on the Staten Island Ferry, stroll through Central Park and cross the Brooklyn Bridge for free. In summer, concert series like Prospect Park's BRIC and the Public's Shakespeare in the Park cost nothing. Dine on pizza from 2 Bros ($1.50 per slice) and stay at a hostel – you'll save big.

MONEY SAVERS
Take advantage of establishments with happy hours (often 4pm to 7pm). Check museum websites for free admission days. Buy theater tickets at the TKTS Booth or try same-day lotteries.

PAYING THE BILL
Restaurants usually bring a receipt or credit card device post meal. Bars might ask you to 'open a tab' and keep your card until you're done – remember to get it back upon leaving.

TIPPING is not optional – only withhold tips if service is outrageously bad.

Restaurant servers 18–25%

Bartenders $1 minimum per drink, $2 per specialty cocktail or 15–20% overall

Taxi drivers 10–15%

Airport & hotel porters $2 per bag, minimum per cart $5

Hotel cleaners $2–4 per night

RESPONSIBLE TRAVEL

Positive, sustainable and feel-good experiences around the city

CHOOSE SUSTAINABLE VENUES

Support zero-waste restaurants like Rhodora Wine Bar is the star of Brooklyn's clean plate club, where nothing goes to a landfill and even food packaging is compostable.

Buy upcycled fashion at Zero Waste Daniel, an East Williamsburg clothing store that makes sustainable statement pieces using cutting-room scraps from the local garment industry.

Take a green tour at the Javits Center, where a one-acre rooftop farm with birds and bees helps offset the building's energy consumption (javitzcenter.com/sustainability/tours).

Forage for food on a whacky, wonderful and informative public park tour with Wildman Steve Brill (www.wildmanstevebrill.com).

Refill empty bottles with shampoo, toothpaste, lotion and more without purchasing one-time-use plastic products at A Sustainable Village.

Above Buskers, Washington Square Park (p95) **Right** Union Square greenmarket

JOSEPH PERONE/SHUTTERSTOCK ©, BLFMR/SHUTTERSTOCK ©

GIVE BACK

Help feed low-income New Yorkers by donating to City Harvest (cityharvest.org) and Citymeals-on-Wheels (citymeals.org).

Learn how to protect NYC's various bird species, including injured and orphaned feathered friends, with Audubon New York (ny.audubon.org).

Make backpacks with food and essentials for people without shelter at Backpacks for the Street (backpacksforthestreet.org).

Protect the local environment by volunteering to paint, clean and rake NYC's public parks, ensuring these spaces are safe for all visitors (nycgovparks.org/events/volunteer).

Tip fantastic buskers (also called street performers) serenading crowds on subway platforms and in places like Washington Square Park.

SUPPORT LOCAL

Support local farmers and artisan bakers by buying their goods at one of NYC's 45-plus **greenmarkets** (grownyc.org). For the most vibrant experience, head to Union Square – where 140 vendors crowd around the north and west sides of the park in peak season, selling their smorgasbord to roughly 60,000 shoppers every Monday, Wednesday, Friday and Saturday. There's plenty of fare for at-home chefs (veggies, meats, cheeses) and selections for outdoor picnics (fruits, breads, sweets, ciders).

LEARN MORE

Honor the original stewards of NYC's landscape by learning about indigenous ancestors at the National Museum of the American Indian (p45).

Explore multicultural neighborhoods like Jackson Heights (p166), where you can travel to foreign lands through food.

Attend a cultural festival, like the African-forward Afribembé Festival (August, p157) or Puerto Rican Day Parade (June).

GET AROUND

Minimize your carbon footprint by choosing transportation alternatives to taxis and cars. Hop on a train: NYC has one of the world's most extensive and reliable public transit networks. Pedal around town: grab a Citi Bike day pass and roll around the city on leg power alone. Walk: the sidewalks are tailor-made for pedestrians; traffic stays to the right.

CLIMATE CHANGE & TRAVEL

Lonely Planet urges all travellers to engage with their travel carbon footprint, which will mainly come from air travel. While there often isn't an alternative, travellers can look to minimise the number of flights they take, opt for newer aircrafts and use cleaner ground transportation, such as trains.

One proposed solution—purchasing carbon offsets—unfortunately does not cancel out the impact of individual flights. While most destinations will depend on air travel for the foreseeable future, for now, pursuing ground-based travel where possible is the best course of action.

The UN Carbon Offset Calculator shows how flying impacts a household's emissions:

The ICAO's carbon emissions calculator allows visitors to analyse the CO2 generated by point-to-point journeys:

RESOURCES

grownyc.org
nycgovparks.org
citymapper.com
citibikenyc.com

ESSENTIAL NUTS-AND-BOLTS

CAR FREE

Avoid renting a car unless you plan on day tripping outside of city limits. Parking is a hassle and traffic is difficult to navigate.

RENTAL DEALS

When renting a car, you'll find better rates at airports or rental stations outside of the city. Take Metro-North somewhere like White Plains for deals.

ROAD RULES

If you're driving in NYC, don't turn right on a red light – it's illegal.

FAST FACTS

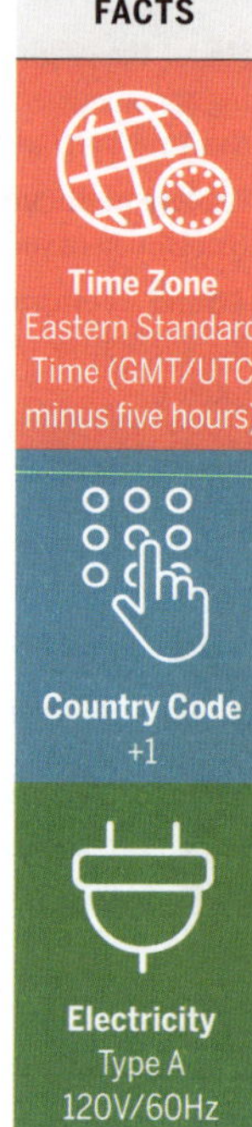

Time Zone
Eastern Standard Time (GMT/UTC minus five hours)

Country Code
+1

Electricity
Type A
120V/60Hz

GOOD TO KNOW

The drinking age is 21 for all establishments selling alcohol. Many bars and clubs will ask for ID upon entry.

Smoking is not allowed indoors, including on public transit, inside train stations, at public parks and within most hotel rooms. It's legal to vape and smoke on streets as long as you maintain distance from building entrances.

For groups larger than four, some restaurants automatically add a tip to the receipt. Check before including more money.

ACCESSIBLE TRAVEL

Dining for all With cramped quarters, many NYC restaurants can be accessibility nightmares. Thankfully, there's **Contento** (p161) – an East Harlem outpost for Peruvian food, built to accommodate wheelchair users.

Sensory-friendly fun Throughout the year, TDF's **Autism Friendly Performance** series presents sensory-friendly productions of Broadway shows, lowering the intensity of lights and sounds for audiences (tdf.org/accessibility-services).

Olfactory adventure Blind and low-vision travelers will find the **Brooklyn Botanic Garden** (p187) a sensorial delight. The **Alice Recknagel Ireys Fragrance Garden**, designed to accommodate visual impairments, allows visitors to touch and smell the flora.

Food for thought In the US, 80% of adults with cognitive disabilities are unemployed. Hungry for change? Grab a bite at Midtown's **Café Joyeux**, working to lower the statistic one employee at a time.

ACCESS TO ADVENTURE
Visit the NYC Tourism website for accessible adventure ideas around town (nyctourism.com/accessible-nyc).

SENSITIVITY FOR SCIENCE
Discovery Squad tours at the American Museum of Natural History guide autistic visitors (amnh.org/plan-your-visit/tours).

ACCESSIBLE EXPERTS
For tips on accommodations and transportation, visit the Accessible Travel NYC blog (accessibletravelnyc.com).

FAMILY TRAVEL

Theater for young audiences The New Victory offers exceptional shows for kids at reasonable prices. Dead set on Broadway? Score discounted tickets to Aladdin or The Lion King on the TodayTix app.

Public playgrounds Let off some steam at one of NYC's 1000 playgrounds. Governors Island, Prospect Park and Central Park are home to some favorites.

Budget experiences Children 11 and under get into the Brooklyn Botanic Garden (p187) for free daily; the Bronx Zoo is free on Wednesdays.

TRANSIT WITH KIDS
Children under 44in ride the subway for free with a fare-paying adult. If you need a stroller, use something light. Elevators and escalators are limited – you'll often have to carry strollers up or down stairs. Buses are a convenient stroller alternative.

PICKY PALATES
There are plenty of children's menus and kid-friendly restaurants throughout town – but for a youth-centered experience, try **Alice's Tea Cup** (a veritable ...Wonderland on the Upper West Side), **Farmacy Soda & Fountain** (Brooklyn's vintage ice-cream parlor) or **Lexington Candy Shop** (p124; try an egg cream).

LGBTIQ+ NEIGHBORHOODS

West Village This is where the first mythic brick was thrown at Stonewall (p91), giving birth to the modern LGBTIQ+ movement.

Chelsea The '90s Chelsea Boy is a daddy now, but he still parties like it's 1999 – especially at the Eagle (p97).

Hell's Kitchen Prepsters and theater kids twirl in bars along Ninth and Tenth Aves.

East Village Manhattan's scruffiest outpost for laid-back LGBTIQ+ folks.

Williamsburg Something for all: lesbian bar Mary's, gay cocktail joint Exley and 3 Dollar Bill (p188) – NYC's biggest queer bar.

Index

M

U

V

W

000 Map pages

'Whenever I see Manhattan's skyline from the Brooklyn Heights Promenade (p182; pictured left), I fall in love with NYC all over again.'

'That time I saw a show at Playwrights Horizons (p103) long before it went to Broadway and became a smash hit.'

'Whenever I spend an afternoon schvitzing with regulars at the Russian & Turkish Baths (p77), followed by a trip to Smør Bakery (p76).'

'The first time I tried the veggie patty from Superiority Burger (p76) and knew I was hooked for life.'

'That time I sailed around Manhattan on a 1920s-style yacht (p83; pictured above right), amazed by the steely urban forestry.'

JOHN GARRY

THIS BOOK

Destination editor
Caroline Trefler

Production editor
Kathryn Rowan

Cartographer
Corey Hutchison

Book designer
Jo-Anne Riddell

Assisting editors
Gabrielle Innes, Kate Mathews

Cover researcher
Kat Marsh

Thanks
Imogen Bannister, Saralinda Turner